DISCARD

DATE DUE

			MAR 1 5 2011

Demco, Inc. 38-293

INVALUABLE
KNOWLEDGE

INVALUABLE KNOWLEDGE

Securing Your Company's Technical Expertise

William J. Rothwell

AMACOM

American Management Association
New York • Atlanta • Brussels • Chicago • Mexico City • San Francisco
Shanghai • Tokyo • Toronto • Washington, D.C.

This publication is designed to provide accurate and authoritative information in regard to the subject matter covered. It is sold with the understanding that the publisher is not engaged in rendering legal, accounting, or other professional service. If legal advice or other expert assistance is required, the services of a competent professional person should be sought.

Library of Congress Cataloging-in-Publication Data

Rothwell, William J.
  Invaluable knowledge : securing your company's technical expertise / William J. Rothwell.
    p.   cm.
  Includes bibliographical references and index.
  ISBN-13: 978-0-8144-1639-6
  ISBN-10: 0-8144-1639-X
    1. Manpower planning.   2. Information technology—Management.   3. Knowledge management.   4. Employees—Recruiting.   5. Employee retention.   I. Title.
  HF5549.5.M3R66155   2011
  658.3'01—dc22
                                                        2010023451

About AMA
American Management Association (www.amanet.org) is a world leader in talent development, advancing the skills of individuals to drive business success. Our mission is to support the goals of individuals and organizations through a complete range of products and services, including classroom and virtual seminars, webcasts, webinars, podcasts, conferences, corporate and government solutions, business books and research. AMA's approach to improving performance combines experiential learning—learning through doing—with opportunities for ongoing professional growth at every step of one's career journey.

Printing number
10 9 8 7 6 5 4 3 2 1

Contents

Preface

Talent management has emerged as a topic of importance. Many organizational leaders are aware that baby boomers around the globe are nearing retirement age. The only thing preventing many of them from retiring now is the long-term influence of fluctuating stock prices. While much attention has been focused on preparing managers for promotion as waves of these baby boomers leave the workforce at some future time, less attention has been devoted to the unique issues associated with losing *knowledge workers*—that is, technical and professional workers whose knowledge is critical to the long-term competitive success of their organizations. Technical and professional workers are essentially "knowledge workers" whose special training, skills, abilities, and experience provide their organizations with competitive advantage.

This book focuses on the unique issues associated with what I call *technical talent management*—that is, the process of attracting, developing, and retaining technical workers (such as engineers, IT professionals, accountants, and finance and investment analysts, whose performance centers on the acquisition and application of knowledge), as well as transferring their knowledge to less experienced workers.

This book consists of nine chapters. Chapter 1 is titled "Introducing Technical Talent Management." It justifies technical talent management as a topic related to, but distinctly different from, traditional views of talent management that focus primarily (and sometimes exclusively) on attracting, developing, and retaining individuals suitable for higher-level responsibility. The chapter also builds a sense of urgency for the book. It explains why organizational leaders and HR professionals should pay more attention to the critical role played by technical and professional workers and how the loss of their unique knowledge might be catastrophic to an organization's competitive advantage. Chapter 2, "Conceptualizing the Issues in Technical and Talent Management," describes the characteristics of effective technical talent management programs, reviews the common mistakes to avoid in implementing such programs, and summarizes some variations in implementing the programs. Chapter 3 offers advice on the unique problems of recruiting and selecting technical and professional workers; Chapter 4 reviews practical approaches to developing these technical and professional workers to achieve their best. Chapter 5 examines how to retain technical and professional workers, while Chapter 6 looks at how to manage and engage these people. Chapter 7 describes theories and models for transferring knowledge, while Chapter 8 lists practical strategies for making this transfer. Chapter 9, the final chapter, offers predictions of challenges that organizations will face in attracting, developing, and retaining this talent, and in transferring the knowledge of workers whose value to their organizations stems from their special expertise.

The book ends with three appendixes. The first consists of case studies to illustrate how organizations have met the challenges of technical talent management. The second appendix is an assessment instrument to help decision makers compare their organizations to best practices for establishing a strategic framework that can support a technical talent management program. The third appendix is an assessment instrument to help decision makers measure how well managers are supporting a technical talent management program on a tactical (that is, daily) basis.

Acknowledgments

I would like to thank my wife, Marcelina, and my daughter, Candice, for just being there for me. Although my son is far away—out there in the cornfields of Illinois—I have not forgotten Froilan Perucho, either.

Thank you to my training session participants, both in the United States and in many other nations, who have shaped my thinking on this topic. A special thanks to my friend Gem Ong at Salvo in Singapore, and to participants in Hong Kong, where I first presented on the topic of this book, and to the many participants in the United States and in many other nations who have participated in my workshops on "technical succession planning," "technical talent management," and related topics. They helped me hone the ideas and realize just how critical is the need for talent management programs distinctly focused on people who possess invaluable knowledge.

I also wish to thank people who reviewed this book in early drafts and offered advice. Thanks to my graduate assistant, Aileen Zabellero, who helped secure the necessary copyright permissions for this book and to others who contributed in some way, such as my students Naseem Sherwani and Smitri Raj.

A special thank-you to Christina Parisi, my editor at AMACOM, for her support and patience in helping this book reach the press.

INVALUABLE KNOWLEDGE

Advance Organizer
50 Questions to Test Your Organization's Technical Talent Management

How well do your organization's leaders attract, develop, and retain its technical and professional workers? And how well does the organization transfer their knowledge to succeeding generations of workers?

Review the following Advance Organizer pretest before you read this book. Use it to help you identify topics of special interest so that you can jump right to the subject that will best address your organization's problems.

Using the Advance Organizer

Read each item in the pretest that follows. Circle **T** (true), **N/A** (not applicable), or **F** (false) in the left-hand column, next to each item. Spend about 20 minutes on this organizer. Be honest! Think of how your organization manages the individuals who possess special knowledge of the work, work processes, customers, technology, and other matters of critical present and future competitive value to your organization. When you finish, score your results, and interpret those results using the instructions at the end.

Then, be prepared to share your responses with others in your organization. Use the results as a starting point for improving the way your organization conducts its talent management for technical and professional workers such as engineers, IT professionals, research scientists, research and development (R & D) workers, and others who possess special knowledge that is invaluable to your business. To learn more about each item on the pretest, refer to the chapter number in the right-hand column, where the subject is discussed in detail.

Has your organization established each of the following, geared specifically to technical or professional workers whose knowledge is critical to the organization's present and future success?

Response	Question: Is (Are) there . . . ?	Chapter in the Book
T N/A F	1. A clear definition of the individuals who possess knowledge that is "business critical" for the present or future competitive success of the organization?	1
T N/A F	2. Awareness of the difference between promotable individuals (HiPos) and in-house experts (HiPros)?	1
T N/A F	3. A compelling sense among decision makers of how important to the future of the business is the knowledge possessed by technical and professional workers?	1
T N/A F	4. A clear understanding of the difference between talent management programs designed to prepare individuals for more responsibility (promotion) and technical talent management programs designed to attract, develop, and retain people who possess unique knowledge and can transfer the experience, knowledge, or competencies of crucial value to business success?	1
T N/A F	5. A clear understanding of the difference between technical talent management and replacement planning for technical or professional workers?	1
T N/A F	6. A clear sense, linked to the organization's strategy, of why a technical talent management program is important?	1

Response			Question: Is (Are) there . . . ?	Chapter in the Book
T	N/A	F	7. A good sense of the importance of a strategic model to guide a technical talent management program?	1
T	N/A	F	8. Measurable goals for a technical talent management program?	1
T	N/A	F	9. Distinct roles in technical talent management that are played by each key stakeholder group?	1
T	N/A	F	10. Ways that each stakeholder group in the technical talent management program will be held accountable for achieving the organizational goals as part of the program?	1
T	N/A	F	11. Identifiable work processes that are critical to the organization's success?	1
T	N/A	F	12. Up-to-date present work duties of importance to technical and professional workers?	1
T	N/A	F	13. Identified technical competencies of knowledge workers?	1
T	N/A	F	14. A way to pinpoint which workers possess the most valuable knowledge (that is, who the HiPros are)?	1
T	N/A	F	15. A means to estimate the risk of losing workers who possess the most valuable knowledge?	1
T	N/A	F	16. Awareness of the need to attract workers who possess special knowledge of value in enhancing the organization's core competence?	1
T	N/A	F	17. A method to align strategic plans with future talent needs?	1
T	N/A	F	18. A plan to implement the technical talent management program by recruiting, developing, and retaining people with special knowledge?	1
T	N/A	F	19. Practical ways to implement knowledge-transfer strategies to get HiPros to help less experienced people learn more of what the HiPros know?	1

Response			Question: Is (Are) there . . . ?	Chapter in the Book
T	N/A	F	20. Practical ways to evaluate the continuing results of the technical and professional talent management program?	1
T	N/A	F	21. Plans to ensure that top managers support the technical and professional talent management program?	2
T	N/A	F	22. Determination of whether top managers are willing to devote resources to the program?	2
T	N/A	F	23. Assurance that the technical talent management program is responsive to the differences between technical/professional workers and management workers?	2
T	N/A	F	24. Guarantees that the technical talent management program recognizes the difference between potential (promotability) and expertise (know-how)?	2
T	N/A	F	25. Assurance that the program focuses on the person, not on the position or hierarchical level?	2
T	N/A	F	26. Belief that the program is based on knowledge of critical business value?	2
T	N/A	F	27. Certainly that the program avoids confusion about why it exists?	2
T	N/A	F	28. Supposition that the program avoids devoting insufficient resources to the effort?	2
T	N/A	F	29. Guarantees that decision makers do not have unrealistic expectations about what can be accomplished in a short time?	2
T	N/A	F	30. A recruiting effort based on the organization's reputation (that is, employment brand) as an employer of choice for technical and professional people?	3

Response	Question: Is (Are) there . . . ?	Chapter in the Book
T N/A F	31. A recruiting effort that recognizes the unique differences in attracting most employees and technical and professional workers?	3
T N/A F	32. A selection effort that recognizes the unique differences in choosing between most employees and technical and professional workers?	3
T N/A F	33. Steps taken to develop an onboarding program for technical and professional workers?	3
T N/A F	34. A development program that informs technical and professional workers what has been learned in the past, what has been learned recently, and what new developments will arise in the future?	4
T N/A F	35. Development programs that emphasize on-the-job learning?	4
T N/A F	36. Encouragement of development and retention by using dual-career ladders?	5
T N/A F	37. Establishment of individual accountability for development?	5
T N/A F	38. Recognition of the disadvantages of dual career ladders and steps to minimize those disadvantages?	5
T N/A F	39. A tactical model to guide managers' contributions to the technical talent management program?	6
T N/A F	40. Clear daily roles for each manager who oversees technical and professional talent?	6
T N/A F	41. Daily accountabilities for each manager in attracting, developing, and retaining technical and professional talent?	6
T N/A F	42. Established management accountability for facilitating transfer of knowledge on a daily basis?	6

Response			*Question: Is (Are) there . . . ?*	*Chapter in the Book*
T	N/A	F	43. A means to measure, on a daily basis, how well each manager carries out his/her role in technical talent management?	6
T	N/A	F	44. Ways to improve what managers do every day so as to contribute to the technical talent management program's success?	6
T	N/A	F	45. Systematic efforts to improve what managers do to cultivate technical and professional talent and transfer valuable knowledge?	6
T	N/A	F	46. Evaluation of efforts to improve managers' cultivation of technical and professional talent and knowledge transfer?	6
T	N/A	F	47. Assurances that knowledge from experience is transferred from those who have gained it to their replacements?	7
T	N/A	F	48. Reliance on multiple methods to encourage knowledge transfer?	7
T	N/A	F	49. Recognition that HiPros will not transfer knowledge unless they see a reason for doing so (what's in it for them)?	7
T	N/A	F	50. Periodic updates of technical talent management programs so as to accommodate likely future trends?	8

Scoring and Interpreting the Advance Organizer

Give *1 point* for each **T** and *0* for each **F** or **N/A**. Total the number of Ts. Then interpret your score as follows:

40 or more   Your organization apparently is using effective technical talent management practices. Although improvements can

be made, the critical success factors for an effective technical talent management program already are in place—assuming, of course, that you answered this assessment honestly and that the score does not merely represent wishful thinking.

39 to 30   Improvements could be made to technical talent management practices in the organization. But, on the whole, the organization is proceeding on the right track.

29 to 20   Technical talent management practices in your organization do not appear to be as effective as they should be. *Significant improvements should be made.*

19 or less   Technical talent management practices are ineffective in your organization. Your organization may be at significant risk of losing invaluable knowledge. *Take immediate corrective action steps.*

1.

Introducing Technical Talent Management

What is your organization doing about the special challenges of recruiting, developing, and retaining technical and professional talent, such as its engineers, IT professionals, accountants, and others who rely on specialized knowledge—knowledge that may be key to your organization's strategic, competitive success? What is your organization doing to transfer the invaluable knowledge these people have to your new hires and to less experienced knowledge workers? Are you preparing for a possible future wave of retirements as the baby boomers leave your workforce? Are you preparing systematically for knowledge workers as your organization grows explosively? How well is your organization managing its knowledge transfer as part of its talent management and succession planning strategies?

Five Mini-Studies: Can You Solve These Problems?

Read the following mini-cases and describe how your organization would meet the challenges you find in each situation. If your organization has ways to solve all of these problems, then perhaps it already has an effective strategy for technical and professional talent management (abbreviated throughout this book as *technical talent management,* or TTM). If your organization could not solve the problems presented below, then your leaders may want to consider a technical talent management program as a means to solving them when they appear.

Mini-Study 1

You analyze the retirement eligibility of your organization's engineering division. Shaking your head, you note that, in five years, about 40 percent of all the engineers in the division will be eligible for retirement. Considering the organization's recent downsizing efforts and early retirement offers, you wonder where the next generation of engineers will come from. Hiring engineers is possible if the compensation is attractive enough—although you are keenly aware that some people believe there is a global shortage of engineers (an opinion not universally shared)—but you know that new hires will not have in their heads the special knowledge of the technical decisions that have been made to reach your company's current generation of high-tech products. How, then, will the new hires be positioned to contribute to the next generation of products if these engineers have never had a chance to learn from experience?

Mini-Study 2

Medical researchers in your organization have spent years pursuing various research plans to perfect new drugs and find cures for many of humankind's worst ills. But recently several of the most prominent medical researchers in your organization have given their supervisors notice that they plan to retire within one year. Your managers wonder how to retain and transfer the knowledge these researchers have before the scientists leave the organization. One idea that decision makers have offered is to keep the researchers on contract for a year or two while they train their replacements. However, the organization's HR policies do not make that easy to do, nor do the retirement plans for which these researchers are eligible. And a one-year effort seems like a Band-Aid placed on an arterial hemorrhage. Even if it is possible—and that is by no means certain—how can a lifetime of learning be transferred in only one year?

Mini-Study 3

Lou Smith is one of those rare people on your company's assembly line who knows every quirk about the machine he has operated for fifteen years. It has been easy to take Lou for granted, since he rarely takes a vacation or calls in sick. In fact, he has been first in line for all the overtime the company would give him. But, overnight you receive word that Lou is in the hospital, having suffered a massive heart attack. Nobody is sure whether he will make it. The supervisor of Lou's assembly line is complaining that, while he has a backup for Lou, that person does not know as well the machine that Lou has made "sing" for years. You worry how much production might be lost while Lou is out sick.

Mini-Study 4

Martha Milhouse knows every decision maker in the high-tech companies she has sold to for over five years. She has been diligent about remembering their birthdays; she knows her stuff, too, and can sit in a product meeting with engineers and understand what they are talking about, even though she is not an engineer. Her combination of good interpersonal skills and grasp of the technical side of the products has made her a top salesperson for the technical products your organization produces. But Martha's husband has just retired; he is pressuring her to do likewise. As sales manager, you wonder how you can find another person who knows the products—and customers—as well as Martha does. And you wonder how many sales will be lost if you do not find that person.

Mini-Study 5

Rhonda Yeager has been a systems analyst with the company for years. People feel that she knows everything about every IT system used by the organization. But Rhonda walked into her supervisor yesterday and, without warning, turned in her resignation. The IT manager was stunned. He shook his head, then he voiced dismay at the prospect of hiring or developing anyone else who could know even a fraction of what Rhonda knows about the IT systems. Some of the systems in IT, the manager knows, are "legacy systems" that have been around so long that nobody else remembers how they work, as there is such limited documentation.

Describing "Knowledge Workers"

Let's be clear on definitions. What is a knowledge worker? And, more specifically, what is a technical or professional worker? A *knowledge worker* is usually understood to be those people who rely on professional judgment or specialized training to perform their work. According to the Bureau of Labor Statistics (BLS),

> the professional, scientific, and technical services sector comprises establishments that specialize in performing professional, scientific, and technical activities for others. These activities require a high degree of expertise and training. The establishments in this sector specialize according to expertise and provide these services to clients in a variety of industries and, in some cases, to households. Activities performed include: legal advice and representation; accounting, bookkeeping, and payroll services; architectural, engineering, and specialized design services; computer services; consulting services; research services; advertising services; photographic services; translation and interpretation services; veterinary services; and other professional, scientific, and technical services.[1]

Technical, scientific, and professional workers are, therefore, those who work in occupations that require specialized knowledge and training. For this sector, average wages are high—averaging $29.78 per hour in the United States in November 2009. According to BLS, 7,605,300 people were employed in this sector in the United States in December 2009, the most recent date for which statistics are available. The number of employers in the sector during the second quarter of 2009 was large: 1,010,967 in private industry, 906 in local government, 401 in state government, and 1,482 in the federal government in the second quarter of 2009.

Defining "Technical Talent Management"

As the mini-studies at the opening of the chapter illustrate, today's leaders need to do more than merely plan for their own replacements. While leadership succession is undoubtedly important, it is just not enough in this current age, when what people know and what they can do are as important as how people can lead or manage. Real-world cases of organizations struggling to deal with an expected "brain drain" have figured prominently in the business press (see Appendix I).

Technical talent management (TTM) is the process that focuses on attracting, developing, and retaining the most talented technical and professional workers and transferring their specialized knowledge to less proficient or less experienced workers. Its goal is not so much to ready people for promotions or vertical mobility in the way management or leadership-oriented talent management does. Instead, it aims to transfer *institutional memory*, defined as the collective wisdom that an organization's members have gained from their experience and that is embedded in its corporate culture.

Technical talent management also aims to transfer *tacit knowledge*, or what people carry around in their heads as a result of their experience and learning. TTM should not be confused with *knowledge management* (KM), an activity that treats knowledge as an important component of business and intellectual assets as critical to achieving business results. TTM can, however, be properly regarded as a subset of KM. Of particular importance to TTM is *knowledge transfer*, meaning the communication of practical business knowledge that has been learned from experience with the work, work processes, people, customers, and business challenges and problems with which the organization deals or has dealt with.

TTM at the organizational level should not stand alone. It should be combined with efforts to focus attention on daily practices by managers to attract, develop, retain, and transfer the knowledge of especially talented knowledge workers. Sophisticated IT-based knowledge management systems and software, while helpful, should not be the only means by which knowledge transfer is managed over time. TTM assumes that most "talent building" does (and should) occur in practical ways and in real time through experiences with people, work processes, customers, typical and special problems, and challenges stemming from the work, as well as any other specialized knowledge of key value to the business.

It is important to distinguish among *data, knowledge,* and *information.* As Boisot observes:

> Think of *data* as being located in the world and of *knowledge* as being located in agents, with *information* taking on a mediating role between them. Data can be viewed as a discernible difference between different energy states only some of which have information value for agents. Where data are thus informative, it will modify an agent's expectation and dispositions to act in particular ways—that is, what we call its knowledge base.[2]

A TTM program is, therefore, a systematic effort to attract, develop, and retain the most knowledge-proficient people while, at the same time, seeking to identify, capture, distill, and transfer specialized knowledge from those who possess that valuable knowledge to others who do not possess it. The TTM focus is not so much on management continuity as it is on ensuring the continuity of knowledge essential to business operations and competitive success and on cultivating knowledge workers and in-house experts who possess special know-how.

Knowledge workers are individuals who have undergone specialized training and who possess unique knowledge that is of value to an organization. In that sense, many people are knowledge workers because participation in organizational life gives people some memory of what happened. And the collective memory of what has happened, and what was learned from it, amounts to *institutional memory*. At the same time, in-house experts—also called *High Professionals* (HiPros)—may not necessarily be promotable up the traditional organizational hierarchy but they are the recognized "go-to" people for solving myriad technical and professional problems. A HiPro can be the one person who knows the most about any one thing of critical value to business operations.

One aim of TTM is to transmit the institutional memory so that mistakes made in the past are not repeated. Without institutional memory, members of an organization would have to keep reinventing the wheel, doing what seems essential to the organization's mission and strategy. As poet and philosopher George Santayana once said, "those who cannot remember the past are condemned to repeat it."[3] And without memory of the past, future workers will not know what to do or how to do it.

Another aim of TTM is to retain and transmit tacit knowledge. Experience is valued precisely because people learn from it. But most practical learning is not taught in school, though education does provide an important basic, theoretical foundation for practical learning on the job. (It would be difficult to imagine doing a job without the abilities to read, write, or work mathematical problems.) Some of what people learn can be easily transmitted—this is called *explicit knowledge*; some learning is not so easily transmitted because it is embedded in the process of gaining the experience—what is called *tacit knowledge*. Without tacit knowledge, people could not have learned from their experiences or their mistakes. Likewise, people can learn *formally* (through planned educational events), *informally* (based on experience), or *incidentally* (based on accidental learning that results serendipitously from experience).

Distinguishing Technical Talent Management from Related Topics

Specialized terms can lead to confusion. For that reason, it just makes sense to begin with some definitions so as to distinguish TTM from other topics with which it may be easily confused.

TTM vs. Replacement Planning

Replacement planning is a form of disaster planning or risk management.[4] To conduct traditional replacement planning, managers are usually tasked to identify emergency backups for themselves in case they are unexpectedly (and disastrously) lost through sudden resignation, disability, sickness, or death. Managers also may be asked to identify possible backups for their immediate reports. The results of traditional replacement planning are usually reviewed by higher levels of management, and perhaps by peers of the manager as well, as a reality check on how likely individuals are to be selected as replacements in an emergency.[5] The final outcome of the process is a replacement chart that identifies who the backups are, how ready they are for emergency promotion, and in what order they should be chosen. If fewer than three backups are identified for each key position, the organization is said to "have holes." A *hole* is an area in which the organization is exposed if something should happen to the present job occupant. When no backups are identified, the organization's leaders may take steps to "fill the hole" by finding understudies.

It is important to emphasize that, in replacement planning, people are not guaranteed promotions simply if they appear on a replacement chart. When their names are listed, it merely means that they can serve as temporary backups until there is time for a proper job search to find a suitable replacement. That may, or may not, result in choosing the person who fills in during the emergency.

According to available research, fewer than 40 percent of U.S. companies have identified emergency backups in case of the sudden loss of key people.[6] That places their organizations at extraordinary risk. If the plane crashes carrying the CEO, or even the entire senior management team, the event can be devastating to the organization. Since passage of the Sarbanes-Oxley Act, enacted by Congress following the Enron scandal to make boards of directors accountable for more than their organizations' financial results, corporate boards have become more aware of the risks posed when an organization does not have replacement plans or succession plans.

Replacement planning charts can be adapted for use in recording the special knowledge, skills, attitudes, or other competencies possessed by workers. Unlike traditional replacement charts, however, competency-based replacement charting does not automatically regard managers as special-knowledge workers. Instead, the key criterion is special expertise that would pose a hardship if its owner is suddenly lost. See Exhibit 1-1 for an example of a replacement chart with slots to note individuals' talents and strengths. Note the assumption here that some people possess knowledge that may be absolutely critical to continued business survival or continuity, and that some provision must be made for their sudden loss.

TTM, therefore, focuses on special knowledge, while replacement planning focuses on backups for people. TTM thus emphasizes the collective knowledge of the organization that is needed to achieve strategic objectives over time. Replacement planning is a crude substitute, but TTM requires a more sophisticated view of what kind of knowledge the organization requires for achieving and sustaining competitive success.

TTM vs. Workforce Planning

Few organizations make a comprehensive comparison between the competencies of existing workers and the requirements posed by the organiza-

EXHIBIT 1-1.

SAMPLE REPLACEMENT CHART FOR TALENT OR INDIVIDUAL STRENGTH.

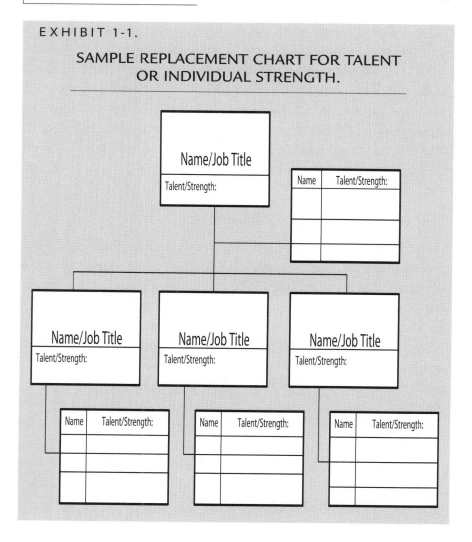

tion's strategy.[7] Instead, a typical norm is "vacancy-by-vacancy" planning, probably because that is the way it has always been done in most organizations. This usually is more common than a big-picture look at how well the collective competencies of all workers match present and future competitive business needs. In addition, more organizations classify workers according to the cost of their wages and benefits or by headcount than according to their unique know-how, talent, or specialized expertise.

TTM requires the organization's leaders to consider the special knowledge and competencies needed for the organization's competitive success. It can include a big-picture look at where the experts are in the organization and what their expertise is, framed in the context of the organization's customers, work processes, products, and practical problems.[8]

TTM vs. Traditional Talent Management

Talent management traditionally has been linked to sourcing the best people, preparing them, and retaining them. But not everyone agrees on the meaning of the term, and that leads to much confusion. Some organizational leaders associate talent management with giving special attention to managing the best-in-class talent of the organization—the upper 1 to 10 percent.[9] Yet, traditional talent management need not be limited to so-called *top-of-the-house planning*, where the focus is solely on finding successors for the senior executive team. Traditional talent management may also include investments in training, education, and development where the financial returns to the business are likely to be greatest—that is, applied to high-performing, highly knowledgeable, or high-potential talent at any level. Hence, efforts to develop talent that is strategically important for the organization's future implies the *strategic development of talent*.[10]

Technical talent management can be viewed simply as a way of attracting, developing, and retaining people in a technical talent pool. The idea is to prepare a large number of people to assume technical or professional positions, but to consider them for their strengths, expertise, or special abilities when making decisions about specific assignments, projects, or promotions. One way to conceptualize it is as a group of people listed by talent, special expertise, or personal strength, and then keyed to leveraging those strengths to advantage. See Exhibit 1-2 for an example

EXHIBIT 1-2.

TYPICAL TECHNICAL TALENT POOL CHART.

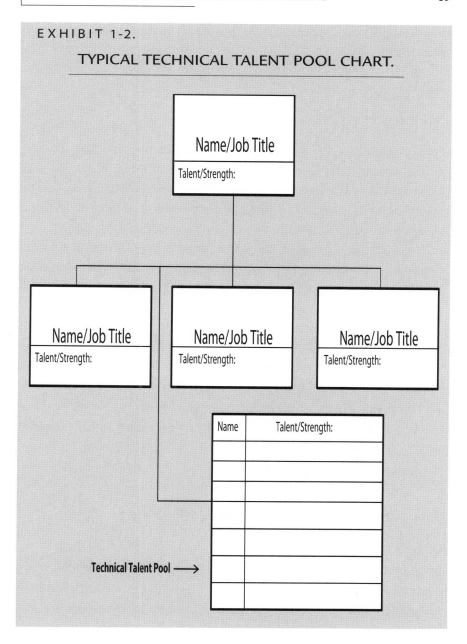

of a technical talent pool chart, with slots for noting individuals' talents and strengths.

Making the Case for TTM

Organizational leaders are surrounded by competing priorities, so it requires a compelling case, based on legitimate business needs, to "sell" technical talent management to them. And, since what leaders see depends on their placement in an organization and what they value, it may be easier to sell TTM to some managers than to others.

Of course, it depends on the type of organization, as well. Some organizations are more dependent on specialized knowledge—its acquisition, analysis, communication, and manipulation—than are others. They use knowledge as an important factor in achieving competitive advantage.

Consider, for instance, high-technology firms like Siemens, Motorola, Microsoft, Apple, or Intel. Without their (enviable) engineering expertise, where would they be? Out of business, most likely. And the same is true of consulting companies such as McKinsey, Booz Allen, and Accenture, which provide expert advice or manage highly specialized projects. There is, thus, a relationship between how well an organization competes and how well it manages its knowledge assets.[11]

A Strategic Model for Technical Talent Management

Most best-practice firms have a strategic model or roadmap that represents all the complicated components of a technical talent management program. These models are considered *strategic* because they are long term and are tied to meeting key business needs and achieving strategic business objectives. They are *integrated* because they show how all the "moving parts" work together to achieve those results. Appendix II will help you consider how your organization rates in the strategic management of technical talent assets.

Exhibit 1-3 is a nine-step strategic model that depicts technical and professional talent management. A good place to start building management awareness of a need for technical talent management is to interview managers at all levels; see the interview guide in Exhibit 1-4, designed for collecting information from managers in the organization.

Step 1: Clarify the Goals, Roles, and Accountabilities

What is the business problem or challenge that the TTM program is intended to address? How can that be converted from a problem to one or more *measurable goals* that serve to guide the program? Clarifying the goals of the program is essential because top managers do not always share the same perspectives. Examples of general goals might include capturing:

- The institutional memory of those who are, or soon will be, retirement eligible

- Special knowledge of products, services, or customers from those who are, or soon will be, retirement eligible

- Special knowledge of work processes and workflow from those who are, or soon will be, retirement eligible

Each goal or target then should be converted to a factor that can be measured according to its quality, quantity, cost, time, or customer satisfaction level. Use the worksheet in Exhibit 1-5 to help obtain agreement from decision makers on the key goals of the TTM program and then how to make those goals measurable. (If the goals are not made measurable, it is difficult to track results.) For example, these goals might be (1) transferring knowledge from those with more expertise to those with less; and (2) preparing for retirements of experienced workers who possess invaluable knowledge.

(text continues on page 24)

EXHIBIT 1-3.

STRATEGIC MODEL FOR TECHNICAL AND PROFESSIONAL TALENT MANAGEMENT.

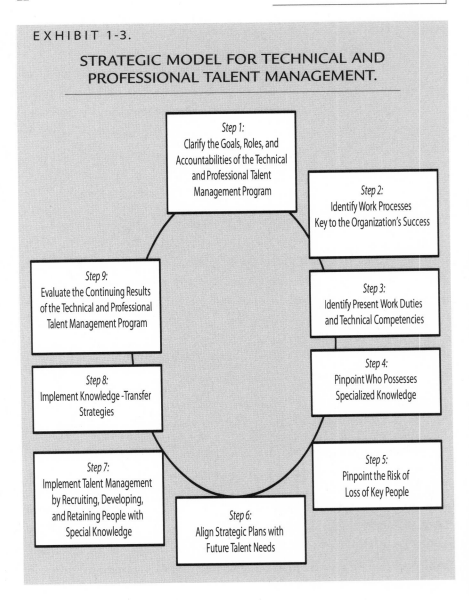

Step 1:
Clarify the Goals, Roles, and Accountabilities of the Technical and Professional Talent Management Program

Step 2:
Identify Work Processes Key to the Organization's Success

Step 3:
Identify Present Work Duties and Technical Competencies

Step 4:
Pinpoint Who Possesses Specialized Knowledge

Step 5:
Pinpoint the Risk of Loss of Key People

Step 6:
Align Strategic Plans with Future Talent Needs

Step 7:
Implement Talent Management by Recruiting, Developing, and Retaining People with Special Knowledge

Step 8:
Implement Knowledge -Transfer Strategies

Step 9:
Evaluate the Continuing Results of the Technical and Professional Talent Management Program

EXHIBIT 1-4.

INTERVIEW GUIDE FOR IDENTIFYING VALUABLE KNOWLEDGE.

Directions: Ask managers in your organization each of the questions below. Take notes or (with permission) tape-record their responses. Then analyze the responses to identify what the managers consider the most valuable knowledge held by people in the organization.

Introduction

Thank you for agreeing to meet with me. The purpose of this interview is to gather your thoughts on the most valuable knowledge in the organization that may be at risk of loss owing to surprise resignations, pending retirements, or accidents such as sudden deaths or disabilities. Think for a moment not about people who are promotable but, rather, who have the most valuable knowledge of the business, its customers, the technology, work processes, machinery, and other components that are critical to the continuity of the business. Think of people who would be tough to replace because they possess unique knowledge gained from experience.

Questions	Answers/Notes
1. What do you believe is the single most important competitive advantage that this organization possesses that gives it a strategic advantage over its competitors? What do we do best? (*Hint:* This is something that should never be outsourced because then that uniqueness would be lost.)	
2. Who knows the most about that competitive advantage you've just cited?	
3. Think of people in your area of responsibility whom you would	

Questions	Answers/Notes
regard as in-house experts, or individuals who possess critically important knowledge. What information do they possess that is so important? How do you know they possess that information?	
4. Which of these in-house experts do you believe might be at greatest risk of being lost? Why do you think so?	
5. What approaches have you already used to transfer the knowledge these in-house experts—those you would call High Professionals—to less knowledgeable, less expert, or less experienced people? How well have those attempts worked out?	
6. What other approaches do you believe would work to transfer this valuable knowledge? Why do you believe so?	
7. How should we evaluate and measure the success of these knowledge-transfer efforts?	

Each stakeholder group in the organization has a role to play, but often no one takes the time to define those roles. Each *role* should involve a list of expected behaviors and results. Examples of stakeholders include the CEO, the senior manager of each group reporting to the CEO, the HR department, the immediate supervisors of technical and professional workers, and the workers themselves. Use the worksheet in Exhibit 1-6 to clarify the roles of each stakeholder group.

Accountabilities also must be clear. How will the stakeholders be held

EXHIBIT 1-5.

WORKSHEET FOR SETTING MEASURABLE GOALS OF A TTM PROGRAM.

Directions: Working either individually or with groups of managers, distribute this worksheet to decision makers so as to help them reach agreement on the desired results of a technical talent management program. Once decision makers reach agreement on goals, they can then agree on the metrics by which to evaluate the program's success.

What should be the goals of the TTM program?

1.

2.

3.

4.

5.

How should each goal be measured and how often should it be measured?

1.

2.

3.

4.

5.

accountable for playing their roles and helping achieve the organization's measurable technical talent management goals? For instance, should knowledge transfer become part of each worker and each manager's key performance indicators (KPIs)? If so, make that an explicit part of each worker's and each manager's job description. Then determine exactly what measurable expectations are to be achieved from them. The measures may have to be discussed, and brainstormed, by the department to

EXHIBIT 1-6.

WORKSHEET FOR IDENTIFYING ROLES OF KEY STAKEHOLDERS.

Directions: Write down the role descriptions for each key stakeholder group involved in the TTM program. List both the activities and how those activities will be measured in terms of accountability. Use additional sheets, if necessary. Review these roles at least annually.

Stakeholder Group	Activities of the Group	Means of Measurement
CEO	Example: Devotes 20 percent of personal time each week to talent management.	
Senior Managers		
Middle Managers		
Front-Line Supervisors		
HR Department		
Individuals		
Other Key Stakeholders		

ensure that knowledge pinpointed for transfer is, indeed, critical to future business success. Not all knowledge is useful or critical, but some knowledge gained from experience, institutional memory, and special knowledge about work processes, equipment, tools, procedures, company products, and customers may be vital to future competitive success. Efforts to transfer that knowledge will break down, however, if these priorities are not established and followed.

Accountabilities should be tied to rewards and/or punishments. For instance, workers or managers who meet or exceed their technical talent management and knowledge-transfer expectations should be eligible for a pay raise or special bonus than would otherwise be the case. Participation in planned programs—such as mentoring—to transfer knowledge should likewise be recognized and rewarded. But how should people be held accountable? Use the activity in Exhibit 1-7 to encourage decision makers to brainstorm ways to hold people accountable for supporting the TTM program. Remember, one approach will not work for all organizations. The approach that is chosen must be one *likely to succeed* in the organization's unique corporate culture.

EXHIBIT 1-7.

ACTIVITY FOR ESTABLISHING ACCOUNTABILITIES FOR THE TTM EFFORT.

Directions: Assemble a small group of 3 to 5 managers. Allocating about 20 minutes, lead a discussion of how managers and workers can be held accountable for a TTM effort. There are no right or wrong answers.

1. How should managers be held accountable for supporting the technical talent management program? *(For example, should it be a measurable key performance indicator? Should part of an annual bonus plan be placed at risk for meeting measurable talent development goals?)*

2. How should technical and professional workers be held accountable for meeting their own technical talent management goals? *(For example, should it be a measurable key performance indicator? Should part of an annual bonus plan be placed at risk for meeting measurable talent development goals? Should superlative efforts be recognized by an organizational program?)*

Step 2: Identify Key Work Processes

A *work process* is usually understood to mean the steps or activities undertaken to complete some work. Examples might include to "hire an employee," "purchase equipment," "manufacture a (specific) product," or "deliver a (specific) service." The term should be familiar to those who have worked with process-improvement efforts or with efforts to install enterprise resource programs (ERPs), such as SAP or Peoplesoft.[12]

There is valuable knowledge embedded in workers' experiences with the work processes that are key to the organization's success. So, to be able to capture and transfer that knowledge, the key work processes need to be identified, which is the second step in the model. The point to note here is that all work processes are not necessarily critical to business success; again, being selective is paramount. If an organization's leaders try to capture all the knowledge workers have of all their work processes, the system will collapse because there will be too much information.

Let's take a simple example. First, identify what the company does better than any of its competitors. If it is Wal-Mart, its key strategic strengths are selling at lowest cost and tracking costs and inventories. If it is Procter & Gamble, its key strategic strength is marketing to consumers. If it is Motorola, its key strategic strength is engineering innovation. In each of these organizations, the goal is to identify the work processes that are tied to the company's key strategic strength—what some would call its *core competency*. It would then be business-critical to identify which employees possess important explicit and tacit knowledge about those processes and who among them might represent risk of loss owing to retirement, illness, or job movement. Transferring their knowledge is critical to future business continuity and success.

Step 3: Identify Work Duties and Technical Competencies

Another way to understand the nature of valuable knowledge is to recognize that it is embedded in the work and functional or technical competencies of certain employees. While traditional talent management and succession planning are interested in general management competencies by hierarchical level—such as the difference between a middle manager and an executive—TTM is interested in specialized work activities and functional or technical competencies by *area*. (Exhibit 1-8 illustrates this difference.) For instance, what are the technical competencies of a mechanical engineer in a particular organization? What specific work activities are carried out by technical or professional workers within the context of that one unique corporate culture?

The theory behind TTM is that valuable tacit knowledge is embedded in specialized work and technical competencies. That is, veteran workers have learned from experience. To ferret out that knowledge, the organization's leaders need to explore what those veteran workers have learned from what they do and the characteristics (competencies) that they demonstrate.

EXHIBIT 1-8.

RELATIONSHIP BETWEEN MANAGEMENT COMPETENCIES AND TECHNICAL/ FUNCTIONAL COMPETENCIES.

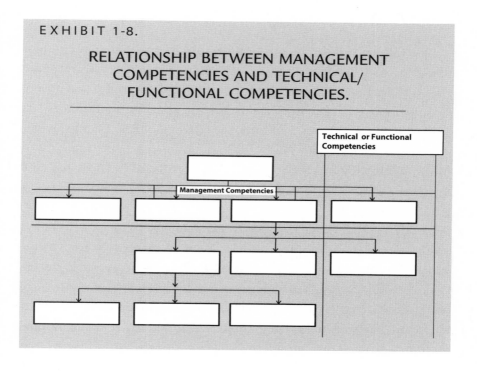

Step 4: Pinpoint Possessors of Specialized Knowledge

Not every worker possesses specialized knowledge. The question is, Who are the organization's in-house experts? It is worth emphasizing here that in-house experts, otherwise called *High Professionals* (HiPros), are not necessarily promotable (nor do they necessarily want to be promoted). But they are the "go-to" people when workers face special problems. They are the most knowledgeable and are likely to know how to solve those special problems.

Few organizations pay much attention to their HiPros. Organizational leaders devote most of their time and attention in talent management or succession planning to finding and developing *High Potentials* (HiPos)—employees who have good job performance and are also perceived to be promotable. But less attention has historically been paid to identifying the good performers who are also the most knowledgeable about a range of subjects affecting the business—such as work processes, equipment, tools, products, customers, or problems unique to the business.[13]

How do most organizations find HiPros? That is an important question, because it is foundational to attracting, developing, and retaining *quality* technical workers. The essence is in grasping exactly what quality is—and how to measure it. Is quality best measured by input factors—as suggested, "such as grade point average at school, highest academic degree earned, major field of study, institution from which the applicant or worker graduated, or years of professional experience?"[14] Or should it be measured by other factors, such as "professional achievements (such as awards, publications, and patents), recent performance review results, demonstrated knowledge in the technical field, ability to apply technical skills as demonstrated by project appraisals or peer reviews by team members on technical teams, demonstrated cross-disciplinary skills, understanding and experience on nontechnical issues (such as management), writing skills, oral presentation skills, willingness to take initiative, creativity and ingenuity on technical projects, commitment to organizational goals, and service orientation?"[15]

An alternative approach is to ask the managers of the technical or professional departments, "Who are your best technical workers, and what makes them the best?" Then you can analyze the results to discover any patterns.

A third approach is to ask individuals within the job categories (such as engineers or research scientists) whom they believe are the "best" people in their field. You can do this by survey, asking participants to list names and explain what makes them "best." Tell them they can name themselves, but that they must still indicate what makes them best. Research indicates that peers, not managers, are really the best judges of which people are the best in class, and the reasons they give are usually realistic measures that could or should be used to assess quality.[16]

A fourth approach to measuring quality is to consider what makes each technical or professional worker unique. What are his or her greatest strengths? What do other people say about that individual regarding the value he or she brings to projects that other people do not—how does the individual achieve results that others do not achieve as well? On what basis would other people seek that person's advice and counsel? The answers may well provide clues to what quality is and what makes the individual's professional expertise unique.

A fifth approach to assessing quality in technical or professional ability is to list all the work activities that a technical or professional worker performs, perhaps using the list of job descriptions in the government's *Dictionary of Occupational Titles*[17] or those listed on the Occupational Information Network (o'net) database.[18] Then you can identify measurable outputs for each work activity. What are the minimum expectations, what are the average outputs, and what are the results of best-in-class workers as objectively measured?

Of course, a sixth approach is to rely on what is termed *expert-finding software*. It exists, and it provides yet another way to pinpoint expertise. This software scans e-mail and then classifies each person according to a frequency count of questions asked, usually by key word. That is a more objective way of identifying in-house experts, but it can be fraught with errors and is certainly not foolproof. (You might imagine what happens when people trade many jokes by e-mail.) But it is one way to start identifying HiPros more objectively than by relying solely on management or worker opinions.

Step 5: Assess Risk of Losing Key People

If it is difficult to pinpoint the in-house experts, it is also difficult to determine which people the organization may be at risk of losing. When someone leaves owing to retirement, resignation, or disability, the organization may lose critical knowledge that could place the company in competitive jeopardy. But if leaders do not even know who possesses special knowledge or they assume everyone represents about the same value to the company, they will fail to recognize the risk of loss from resignation, retirement, disability, or other reasons people leave jobs.

But, of course, once the knowledgeable people are identified, it is possible to assess the risk of their loss. A good place to start is with retirement eligibility. Who is retirement eligible and when? Who is unhappy and may seek alternative employment? What knowledge will the organization lose if those people resign or retire when eligible? These questions should be considered at talent review meetings with equal importance as those given to identifying high potentials, assessing their risk of loss, and planning for their development.

Step 6: Align Strategic Plans with Future Talent Needs

The knowledge that is viewed as business critical may change over time, depending on the organization's strategic direction. Some knowledge may actually grow less important over time while other knowledge may grow more important.

A simple example may illustrate the point. Suppose a retail firm is competing with Wal-Mart and has done a good job of setting itself apart from its bigger rival by specializing in some high-margin goods, such as electronics. The employees who possess the knowledge of what customers want to buy, are able to source those goods at a price at or below Wal-Mart's, and can get them on the store shelves faster will help the organization succeed. But, of course, that requires specialized knowledge of the electronics industry, of the company's major competitor, of suppliers, and of shippers.

Additionally, the products that customers want to buy do not remain the same. In fact, consumer preferences change quickly. Consequently, sustaining a competitive advantage hinges on the ability of the company's buyers to keep ahead of its giant rival. It is the knowledge that those employees have that will sustain competitive advantage. So, the organization's leaders need to clarify *what* knowledge is required in the future to realize strategic objectives. How is that knowledge the same as in the past and how is it different? Who possesses it? How can it be transferred to other employees? These questions need to be answered if the business strategy is to be successfully executed.

Step 7: Recruit, Develop, and Retain People with Special Knowledge

The TTM program will need to include all methods of sourcing talent possessing special knowledge. Some knowledge can be found inside the firm. Some knowledge will have to be recruited externally. Individuals will need to be developed by giving them the experience to gain that knowledge. And once the investment is made to build their experience, they must be retained.

A technical talent management program will not look the same as a leadership development program because the former's focus is on knowledge sharing rather than on preparing people for promotion. The TTM program may include the shadowing of in-house experts by those who possess less knowledge of the business and the specialized knowledge essential to business success. It will probably have to be coordinated by an in-house expert who understands the most critical knowledge that needs to be transferred.

There are occasions when efforts to recruit, develop, and retain people with special knowledge will have to be accelerated. In one public utility, for example, it was determined that all the members of a critically important division were already retirement eligible. They could have chosen to retire at the same time! The board of directors was told of the matter, and they approved the hiring of one individual to shadow each member of the department, but that required doubling up jobs for a year. This approach is called an *acceleration pool process.*[19]

Step 8: Implement Knowledge-Transfer Strategies

An important emphasis in any TTM program is to identify and implement *practical* knowledge-transfer strategies. While fancy (and expensive) knowledge-management software exists, it sometimes disappoints users, for the simple reason that it may be cumbersome and expensive to establish and its results may prove to be disappointing. More practical knowledge-transfer strategies—such as storytelling based on critical incidents—may have to be used that require getting people to talk to each other.[20] These interpersonal approaches can be complicated, since those who possess valuable knowledge may worry that if they reveal what they know, they may no longer be needed.

Step 9: Evaluate the Continuing Results

Evaluation has become one of the most important topics in succession planning and talent management.[21] Leaders often wonder if they are getting their money's worth from the investments made in such programs. And it is not unusual to hear skeptical senior leaders ask for return-on-investment information about these programs—which rarely exists.

But, of course, if the goals established at the outset of the program are clear and measurable, it should be relatively easy to track results. On the other hand, if the goals are vague—as is, unfortunately, too often the case—then decision makers may not be able to see what results were obtained or even agree on their value. The moral is clear: Set measurable goals early on. And then track against them and feed the results back on a continuing basis to decision makers so as to sustain their involvement and commitment.

As business conditions change, the goals of the TTM program also may change. For instance, instead of focusing on knowledge transfer, the program may shift to stimulating innovation. Thus, it may be necessary to recalibrate the goals on a regular basis—such as annually—to ensure that the program continues to meet identifiable organizational needs. Failure to adjust as necessary will lead to the eventual termination of any program.

Chapter Summary

This chapter defined the categories of *knowledge workers* and *technical/ professional workers*. It defined *technical talent management* (TTM) as the process that focuses on attracting, developing, and retaining the most talented technical and professional workers and transferring their specialized knowledge to less proficient workers. Organizations that depend on specialized knowledge need TTM programs the most, though managers will usually have to be convinced of that need.

Both strategic and tactical models are needed to implement effective TTM programs. As this chapter explained, a *strategic model* examines the "big picture." A *tactical model*, treated in a later chapter, focuses on what each manager should do every day to attract, develop, and retain talent and transfer invaluable knowledge. This chapter described each step in a strategic model to guide TTM.

2.

Conceptualizing the Issues in Technical Talent Management

What issues surface as an organization's leaders try to conceptualize and implement a technical talent management program? This chapter addresses that question. It describes the characteristics of effective technical and professional talent management programs, reviews the common mistakes to avoid in implementing such programs, and summarizes some variations in implementing them.

Effective Technical Talent Management Programs

What are the characteristics of effective TTM programs? Very little research has been conducted to answer this question.[1] One reason is that most organizations at present focus their attention primarily, and often exclusively, on talent management to build the leadership bench. There has been, for the most part, a profound absence of attention to systematic efforts to attract, develop, and retain the best technical and professional workers and to transfer their invaluable knowledge to less experienced workers. One study found, for instance, that fewer than 40 percent of U.S. companies make any effort whatsoever to capture the knowledge of experienced workers—their tacit knowledge, gained from experience—before they leave for retirement.[2] Yet two authors have observed, on a related note, that "institutional memory loss is a significant problem that can impact an organization's ability to advance its mission successfully, its ability to avoid making the same mistakes it made in the past, and its ability to leverage the accomplishments of departing employees."[3]

The point even has been emphasized that one reason the United States has not put people on the moon in recent years is that the nation has forgotten how. All of the engineers involved in the original moon missions have since retired. That means, to put someone on the moon, it would be necessary to start from scratch. How many organizations are in danger of making similar mistakes?

It is not such a stretch of the imagination to assume that outstanding TTM programs would meet certain standards and possess certain definable characteristics.[4] Use Exhibit 2-1 to brainstorm how you would answer this question: What characteristics do you believe are critical for a successful program to attract, develop, and retain the best technical and professional workers and to transfer their valuable knowledge to less experienced workers? When you are finished, review the six characteristics of successful TTM programs presented below to see how many points you agree on—and how many are different from your brainstorming.

Characteristic 1: Top Managers Support the Program

While some CEOs and other senior managers may see the need for—and devote attention to—succession planning or talent management efforts geared to building promotable talent, fewer see the need to focus atten-

EXHIBIT 2-1.

ACTIVITY FOR IDENTIFYING CRITICAL CHARACTERISTICS OF TTM PROGRAM.

Directions: Assemble a group of decision makers and ask this question: "What characteristics are critical for a program to attract, develop, and retain the best technical and professional workers, and to transfer their valuable knowledge to less experienced workers?"

If helpful, interview decision makers individually and then present their points of agreement in a meeting. Or assemble small groups of technical and professional workers to brainstorm their own answers to this question.

tion on the special issues associated with managing technical and professional talent. However, there are notable exceptions. CEOs who started out in technical and professional fields are often most keenly aware of—and supportive of—TTM programs. Indeed, in some cases they are *more* supportive of TTM programs than they are of leadership-development efforts, simply because they have greater personal sensitivity to the value that technical and professional workers bring to meeting the strategic objectives of the organization.

Characteristic 2: Top Managers Devote Resources to the Program

It is one thing to pay a program lip service; it is quite another to be willing to devote time, money, and personal effort to the program. Top managers who are committed to TTM are also *personally involved* in attracting, developing, and retaining the technical and professional talent. They are willing to encourage those who report to them to do likewise. They do not delegate the task completely to HR or to an external consultant.

Characteristic 3: There Is Recognition of the Difference Between Technical/Professional Workers and Management

Technical and professional workers do not always want the same things as do the people who work in management. While those who look to vertical promotions may seek exalted titles or higher pay, technical and professional workers often see their employers as providing challenges and resources to keep their skills current, as well as hone those skills to meet future demands.

While it is dangerous to stereotype technical and professional workers, research has uncovered what motivates members of various technical and professional groups. For instance, one researcher concluded that engineers, as a group, are more motivated by the challenge of the work, by recognition from their supervisors, and by professional development opportunities than are people working in other occupational categories.[5] Another study found statistically significant differences in motivation between men and women engineers and among various types of engineers.[6]

Research scientists are, like engineers, chiefly motivated by professional curiosity, a desire to do research, and to analyze, explore, and solve compelling problems; and they want to be recognized by their professional peers for their contributions. Many detest routine administrative work and bureaucratic red tape. Their view of excitement is to solve an engrossing problem on their own, or as part of a team of kindred spirits, and not to sit through endless (and sometimes pointless) management meetings.[7]

It is not difficult to see that successful recruitment, development, and retention programs for most technical and professional workers should emphasize the professional challenges they face—and ensure that they continue to be challenged as they were promised at time of hire.

Characteristic 4: There is Recognition of the Difference Between Potential and Expertise

Traditional talent management programs often classify workers using a grid that places people relative to *performance* (in the current job) and *potential* (for advancement to higher levels of responsibility), as shown in Exhibit 2-2.

Potential in this context refers to a perceived capability to be promoted, or "promotability." High Potential (HiPo) workers are usually those rated high on current job performance and also on perceived potential for advancement. They are the focus of most talent-management ef-

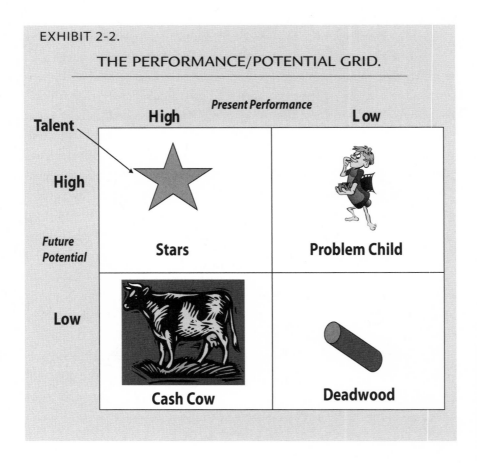

EXHIBIT 2-2.

THE PERFORMANCE/POTENTIAL GRID.

forts, though some people argue that everyone has a talent that could be unleashed if detected and cultivated. Problem employees are perceived to have the potential for promotion but are not performing well in their current jobs. Cows (people who may also be called cash cows or solid performers) should be left where they are but given sufficient training and development to remain productive. Deadwood should be eliminated during downsizing efforts, early-out offers, and other ways to move them out.

But rating employees according to special expertise is different from rating them according to promotability. Yet rating by special knowledge, talent, or expertise is more attuned to TTM. Again using the grid, we see that the performance side remains the same, but the potential side is replaced by "unique knowledge that is key to business success." See Exhibit 2-3 for an example of this grid.

In this version of the grid, HiPros are individuals with demonstrated track records of successful job performance coupled with a high degree of knowledge believed to be key to business success. As a simple example, an engineer whom everyone agrees is the best at troubleshooting a specific problem would be a HiPro for troubleshooting. Similarly, a machinist who is particularly good at working with specific metal surfaces would be regarded as a HiPro for that skill.

Individuals with track records of unsuccessful job performance but who still possess critical knowledge are called LoPros. They are loose cannons; they are the bane of every technical manager because they are mavericks, going their own way, doing their own thing, and they may not be especially helpful in team efforts. Their unique knowledge makes them just valuable enough to keep around, but their performance problems make them difficult to work with.

Individuals with successful track records but who do not possess special knowledge are just Pros. They are usually the newly hired and often are fresh graduates. They have the basic technical or professional knowledge and the rudimentary training, but they do not bring any added value to the organization or to their work. In fact, their work can sometimes be outsourced.

EXHIBIT 2-3.

THE PERFORMANCE/KNOWLEDGE GRID.

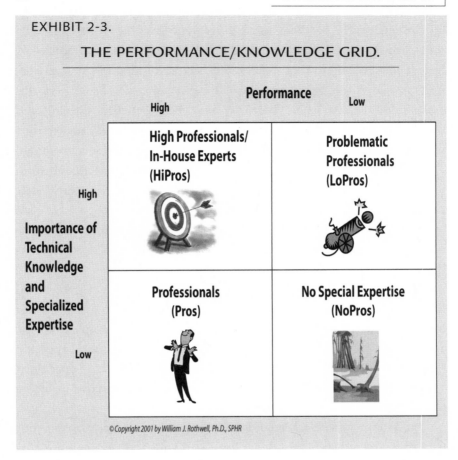

Performance

High   Low

| High Professionals/
In-House Experts
(HiPros) | Problematic
Professionals
(LoPros) |
| Professionals
(Pros) | No Special Expertise
(NoPros) |

Importance of Technical Knowledge and Specialized Expertise

High

Low

© Copyright 2001 by William J. Rothwell, Ph.D., SPHR

Those who have an unsuccessful track record and who also lack knowledge of special value are called NoPros. They add little value to the business, and they are targets for the next round of downsizing or outplacement, as well as early-out offers or employee buyouts. (Think of the character Wally in the Dilbert cartoons and you have an idea of a NoPro.)

Each group requires a different human resources strategy. The knowledge of HiPros should be leveraged and transferred. The LoPros should not be left in the cell where they are—coaching, counseling, and other management actions should move them to another cell, preferably to the HiPros. The Pros need training, planned experiences, and challenges to become HiPros. And the NoPros should be moved to other places where they have the possibility of becoming HiPros or else they should be terminated through downsizing or correct action.

Characteristic 5: TTM Focuses on the Person, Not on the Position or Hierarchical Level

Valuable knowledge is not limited to supervisors, managers, or executives. In fact, the most valuable technical and professional knowledge rests with the people closest to the business challenges. They are often individual contributors—that is, people who do not supervise others. Efforts to transfer knowledge must, thus, necessarily begin with the people who possess it.

Characteristic 6: TTM Is Based on Knowledge of Critical Business Value

As has been said, not all knowledge is worthy of transfer. Not all knowledge is critically important to business success. Consequently, an important challenge for TTM is to pinpoint exactly what knowledge is worth retaining and passing on.

There is more than one way to do that. One way is to break the organization down according to its work processes rather than according to its business hierarchy. This is easier for organizations that have undertaken process-improvement efforts. In so doing, the business processes absolutely critical to business success have been tied to the strategic objectives and to the core competency of the business, setting it apart from its competitors. As that knowledge is mission critical, you know it really must be preserved. And it should never be outsourced because it is key to what makes the business successful.

A second way to identify critical knowledge is to break down the organization according to technical or functional competencies. A technical or functional competency is tied to the unique work of a particular part (silo) of the organization. Technical and professional experts possess special competencies in their fields, and those competencies are mission critical for the silo. One way to think of this is that there are some people who are the absolute best for *each* technical competency, or even for specific behaviors or results tied to each technical competency. They may be regarded as HiPros.

Other Characteristics of a TTM

Exhibit 2-1 was an activity that resulted in a list that will have pinpointed other characteristics that would be important for a TTM program. The final list should be based on what is important to your business leaders. Use the worksheet in Exhibit 2-4 to brainstorm ways your organization can establish a technical talent management program that is consistent with the desirable characteristics.

Common Mistakes and Missteps to Avoid

You may face many problems as you try to implement a technical talent management program. Here are some of them and what you may have to do to solve them.

Problem 1: Confusion About the Program

It is apparent to many senior managers, as they look at the graying heads around the senior management table, that retirements are pending. (In Asia, the problem is having too few people ready to support growth.) And it may not be immediately apparent where the successors are to come from, especially if the organization has been rocked by repeated waves of downsizing. Thus, many organizations have launched succession-planning and talent-management programs. And most have done so because they need people to assume the leadership positions as the senior managers retire.

EXHIBIT 2-4.

WORKSHEET FOR DEVELOPING A CONSISTENT TTM PROGRAM.

Directions: Assemble a group of top managers, technical managers, or even workers in technical and professional jobs. With them, brainstorm ways that your organization can establish a technical talent management program consistent with desired results. For each characteristic listed in the left-hand column below, indicate in the right column what will be done to ensure that the result is achieved via the TTM program. There are no right or wrong answers, per se, but some answers may be better than others.

Characteristic of an Effective TTM Program	*How Will This Be Achieved?*
1. Top managers support the program	
2. Top managers are willing to devote resources to the program	
3. The program is responsive to the differences between technical and professional workers and management workers	
4. The program recognizes the difference between potential and expertise	
5. TTM focuses on the person, not on the position or hierarchical level	
6. TTM is based on knowledge of critical business value	
7. Other characteristics	

But the senior managers may not distinguish between the need to prepare leadership talent for promotion and the need to transfer specialized knowledge, let alone consider the special issues associated with attracting, developing, and retaining the best technical and professional workers. For this reason, some confusion may exist about the differences.

Indeed, HR practitioners and/or the executives in charge of technical and professional areas may have to explain the need for TTM programs and how the focus of such programs differs from general leadership programs. Of course, the two need not be mutually exclusive. It may be possible to have a leadership track and a technical/professional track for fast-track workers. But care should be taken to avoid confusion over what those are and what they mean.

Problem 2: Lack of Resources

The resources may be lacking for proper oversight of technical talent management programs. It may be tough to make the case to senior managers, who are typically removed from daily operations, unless they come from the technical and professional ranks. One way to make the case is to show the differences in contributions—such as numbers of patents filed—by some technical people compared to others. That may dramatize the point that people may be created equal but do not equally contribute.

Problem 3: Unrealistic Sense of Urgency

Typically, if organizational leaders are convinced of the need to act on a TTM program, they may have unrealistic expectations about how quickly action can be taken and how soon results can be obtained. It is not reasonable to assume that results can be achieved with a snap of the fingers or the wave of a magic wand. Essential groundwork must be laid. Measurable goals must be established, roles determined, and a framework for accountability set up so that those with the responsibilities will carry them out. Technical competency models may need to be established. Job descriptions may need to be updated. Approaches to transferring the invaluable knowledge may need to be reviewed by a task force and priorities will need to be established.

Use the worksheet in Exhibit 2-5 to plan for overcoming these and other problems that are so common in establishing and implementing a TTM.

Variations on Program Implementation

Programs to attract, develop, and retain technical and professional workers, as well as to transfer their knowledge, can take many forms and shapes. There is no one right way—indeed, there are many right ways.

EXHIBIT 2-5.

WORKSHEET FOR OVERCOMING IMPLEMENTATION PROBLEMS FOR TTM PROGRAM.

Directions: Assemble a group of top managers, technical managers, or even workers in technical and professional jobs. Brainstorm ways that your organization will be able to avoid or overcome the most common problems in establishing and implementing a technical talent management program. For each problem listed in the left column below, indicate in the right column what you propose as a means to avoid or overcome the problem. There are no right or wrong answers per se, but some answers may be better than others.

Common Problems Affecting TTM Programs	*How Your Organization Will Avoid or Overcome the Problem*
1. Confusion about the program	
2. Lack of resources for the program	
3. An unrealistic sense of urgency	
4. Other problems	

What is essential, however, is that managers are made aware of the need and you enlist their support, you clarify their roles, you establish measurable program goals, and you evaluate the results.

One approach to implementation is to start by activity. For instance, you pick recruitment and selection, and examine ways to improve the onboarding (socialization of newcomers) of technical and professional workers. Alternatively, you can focus on establishing technical/professional career ladders and identify the continuum of competencies in core businesses. If turnover of technical and professional staff is a problem, then you can focus on retention. If knowledge transfer is a need, then you can focus attention on ways to do that—including ways to encourage experienced workers to share what they know.

Another approach is to start with areas of highest possible risk to the business. Conduct a labor-force study of which technical and professional areas have the largest number of people eligible to retire during rolling three-year periods. For example, a rolling three-year period could be 2011–2013; 2012–2014; and so forth; if management prefers, use rolling five years. Periods, rather than specific years, should be examined because trends can be more easily spotted. Then approach the managers of the areas with the highest risks of losing people to retirement. These managers may be more supportive—and more willing to be involved—than if they hear about comprehensive efforts rolled down from the top of all the technical departments in the business at once. It is better to work with managers who see the need and are willing to provide hands-on support than it is to try to work with everyone, as some will not see a need or lack commitment.

Chapter Summary

This chapter described the six characteristics of effective technical and professional talent management programs:

1. Top managers support the program

2. Top managers devote resources to the program

3. The program recognizes the differences between technical/professional workers and management

4. The program recognizes the difference between potential and expertise

5. TTM focuses on the person, not on the position or hierarchical level

6. TTM is based on knowledge of critical business value

The chapter also reviewed three common mistakes to be avoided in implementing such programs and offered suggestions on how to avoid them:

1. Confusion about the program

2. Lack of resources

3. Unrealistic sense of urgency

Finally, the chapter summarized some different ways to get started implementing a TTM program.

3.

Recruiting and Selecting Technical and Professional Workers

Managers and HR professionals who recruit talented technical and professional workers can attest to the unique differences between attracting the best people in these groups and attracting people from other occupations. The ways to build an effective "employment brand" also are different when dealing with members of these groups. Thus, hiring the best people for technical and professional jobs calls for innovative recruitment and selection strategies, not the well-known (and sometimes overused) methods used for filling other positions.

But just what *is* unique about recruiting and selecting technical and professional workers? What should be in a recruitment strategy for these people? How can an organization build a powerful employment brand with technical and professional workers? And how should technical and professional workers be selected? How should they be onboarded? Lastly, how can recruitment and selection be used as a tool to replace invaluable knowledge? This chapter addresses these important questions.

A Recruitment Strategy

Every best-practice firm has devised a recruitment strategy. It is not a short-term plan, created to fill openings as vacancies occur. It is, instead, a long-term plan that pinpoints the organization's continuing and projected recruiting needs, which is based on its expansion requirements (when they exist) and its replacement requirements (stemming from expected retirements). A recruitment strategy thus should answer these important questions:

- What are the business challenges ahead that will influence recruitment?

- Who should be recruited to meet those challenges?

- What particular talents are sought? (The more specifically stated, the better)

- When will the talents be required?

- Where will the talents be used and how will they be applied?

- Why are the talents needed?

- How will the recruiting effort be conducted and what are the justifications for choosing that way?

- How much will the recruitment effort cost and what are its measurable benefits?

- How will special groups (such as protected-class employees) be sought?

A recruitment strategy serves to focus the organization's recruiting efforts. It provides the necessary time to source the applicants and to identify the special initiatives that will encourage certain groups (such as protected-class employees) to apply. It may also allow time to try out interns.

The Unique Challenges of Recruiting and Selecting Technical/Professional Workers

Recruiting and selecting technical and professional workers involves some special challenges that begin with consideration of the people drawn to those occupations. While there is always the risk of stereotyping, and remembering that there can be dramatic differences among the individuals in a group, it is probably no exaggeration to say that technical and professional workers are drawn to their occupations by virtue of their high level of curiosity and their problem-solving, analytical natures. At the same time, they do not (usually) have particularly good interpersonal skills; that preoccupation with solitary analysis sometimes clashes with a sensitivity to dealings with people.

The important point here is that recruiting technical and professional people requires exciting them about the intellectual challenges the organization has that need to be met, the analytical methods that need to be used to solve the organization's problems, and the new technologies that may be sampled in the process of solving those problems. The people in technical fields are interested in the problems in their own right, in their personal sense of satisfaction to be gained by solving those problems, and in the intellectual stimulation they get from applying new approaches and using new technology. They also like to be in touch with the latest thinking, work with the most intellectually stimulating people, be given the most exciting opportunities to apply what they have learned or to learn something new, and experiment with the latest technology and software in their field of endeavor.

A Powerful Employment Brand

An *employment brand* is the reputation that an employer—or part of an organization—enjoys in the labor market. It is something distinct from the employer's brand name. For instance, GE has a particular reputation as a company with its customers but could have an entirely different reputation as an employer.

An organization's employment brand is important because individuals are attracted to work in organizations that match their self-image. That is, if people see themselves as altruistic, they are inclined to work for organizations with a reputation for serving others—such as a non-profit like the American Red Cross, the Salvation Army, or UNICEF. If people see themselves as stimulated by making money, they will be attracted to financial institutions, where money is a mark of achievement. If people enjoy helping others realize their potential, they will be drawn to institutions that foster education, like schools or publishers. If people enjoy helping others maintain their physical well-being, they will be drawn to healthcare.

But even within their fields, employers do not have identical reputations. Some employers have better reputations as places to work than others. A key to recruiting good technical and professional talent is establishing and maintaining a reputation as an employer of choice in the targeted fields, such as engineering, research science, or IT.

Researching the Organization's Employment Brand

How can you determine your organization's employment brand? First, you can conduct a research study among employees in your organization. Contact the workers in your targeted group, and ask them what they feel are the most appealing aspects of working in their profession at your organization. Unlike exit interviews that focus on why people leave, surveys of employment branding identify why people stay, as well as what attracted them to your organization to begin with.

For instance, pick a group of about twelve HiPros and ask them these questions:

◆ Was there a time when you felt particularly excited and energized in your job as a [insert name of occupation] in this organization?

♦ What happened? Explain the situation step by step.

♦ Who was involved?

♦ When did this happen?

♦ Where did this happen?

♦ What made the situation so challenging and exciting for you?

Use the questionnaire in Exhibit 3-1 and send it by e-mail or, if you prefer, ask the questions in face-to-face interviews.

When you have the results, analyze them for common themes, an

---

EXHIBIT 3-1.

QUESTIONNAIRE FOR DEFINING THE ORGANIZATION'S EXTERNAL EMPLOYMENT BRAND.

Directions: Ask 12 HiPros in your organization the following questions. If possible, tape-record their responses. Look for common themes. How many times is the same feature mentioned? Ideas mentioned more than once are indicative of an employment brand.

Questions	Answers
1. Tell about a time you felt particularly excited about your job here. What happened? Explain the situation step-by-step.	
2. Who was involved?	
3. When did this happen?	
4. Where did this happen?	
5. What made the situation so challenging and exciting for you?	

approach called *thematic analysis.* This technique is commonly used to analyze stories for competencies, but it can be applied for other purposes, as it is here for pinpointing the employment brand. For example, what did most people say about what made the situation challenging? The answers to that question shed light on what makes it challenging to work in the organization. This is the nascent employment brand that can be confirmed by follow-up interviews.

It is also possible to distinguish your organization's employment brand by its kinds of workers. For instance, pose the same questions to the HiPros and to the fully successful (average) professionals to discover what attracted them initially and what keeps them in the organization. It is likely that there will be some similarities—as well as some differences—between the groups' responses. When recruiters know what differently attracts HiPros and average performers, then it is possible to craft recruiting strategies that will yield more HiPros.

It is also possible to form a task force including both managers and workers to find effective ways to intensify the important payoffs to the work that attracted people and that keep them. It thus becomes possible for the organization to do two things at once: produce the work and give people more opportunities to experience the feelings of satisfaction that they most want from their jobs. That result yields higher morale and lower turnover and will ultimately attract future talent.

External vs. Internal Employment Brands

There is a difference between an external and an internal employment brand. An *external* employment brand is the reputation that one employer has when competing with other employers for the same talent. An *internal* employment brand is the reputation of one department or one manager in the organization compared to other departments or other managers in the organization.

What is your organization's reputation as an employer? What do people say about your company when employees of the organization are not there? What do former employees tell people about your company? These are all components of an external employment brand. In contrast, what do employees say about working in a specific department? What do they like about it? What do they wish was different? What do employees say about working for one manager compared to others? These are components of an internal employment brand.

Among the questions to ask employees in internal employment branding are:

- How well do you feel that you were oriented to the department?

- How quickly were you challenged by the work in the department?

- How challenging do you find the work in your department?

- What does your manager do to challenge you in your work?

- What could your manager do to improve the challenge you get from the work you do?

- What do your coworkers do to challenge you in your work?

- What could your coworkers do to improve the challenge they give you in your work?

- What opportunities are you given to develop your professional or technical skills that you believe are unique to your department or work group?

Pose these or similar questions in a questionnaire or to a focus group, if you wish. A tool to facilitate doing that can be found in Exhibit 3-2. Use the results as a starting point for improving the organization's internal employment brand and for intensifying the satisfaction that technical and professional workers obtain from working for the company.

EXHIBIT 3-2.

QUESTIONNAIRE FOR DEFINING THE ORGANIZATION'S INTERNAL EMPLOYMENT BRAND.

Directions: Assemble a group of employees and ask the following questions. If possible, tape-record their responses. Look for common themes. How many times is the same feature mentioned? Subjects mentioned more than once are indicative of an employment brand.

Questions	Answers
1. How well do you feel that you were oriented to the department?	
2. How quickly were you challenged by the work in the department?	
3. How challenging do you find the work in your department?	
4. What does your manager do to challenge you in your work?	
5. What could your manager do to increase the challenges you get from your work?	
6. How do your coworkers challenge you in your work?	
7. What could your coworkers do to increase the challenges they give you in your work?	
8. What opportunities are you given to develop your unique professional or technical skills?	

Recruitment and Selection Processes for Technical/ Professional Workers

Once an organization's leaders have successfully built a reputation for being an employer of choice for a targeted group, then the next step is to apply creative approaches to the recruitment and selection of technical and professional workers. But what is special about recruiting these technical and professional workers? How can that recruitment be done creatively? How are the best technical and professional workers selected?

What Is Special About Technical/Professional Workers?

If you have determined what attracts and what motivates your organization's technical and professional workers, then you are well positioned to recruit and select future technical and professional workers. The employment brand can be a theme for recruitment messages, such as those appearing on Web sites, in promotional materials such as recruiting brochures, and in other information directed to applicants. The employment brand should be keyed *realistically* to what attracts workers to the organization.

As a simple example, if workers are attracted to an organization because of the top-quality training it provides, then the recruitment literature could describe that training—and provide testimonials from people in the field who have taken advantage of that training. Similarly, recent hires can be tasked to write blogs of their most memorable experiences in the organization, which serves to dramatize the realistic challenges that new hires face.

The recruiters themselves should possess the technical or professional competence necessary if they are to do anything more than the most rudimentary screening. They must be able to ask detailed questions about courses completed in school, grades obtained (since lower grades in technical fields are more common than in the humanities or liberal arts), experiences the applicant has had (school projects, previous work, or internships), and what the applicant feels he or she can produce for the company. It is not recommended that HR practitioners recruit at colleges or do screening entirely on their own unless they possess the requisite technical education or licensure.

One way to shore up that weakness in recruiting is to take technical professionals—preferably HiPros themselves—along on recruiting ventures or else involve technical workers in the screening. HiPros are useful because they represent the organization's best technical skills and are likely to favor people who are somehow like themselves—a useful bias when the search is on for talented technical or professional workers.

It is not enough to screen technical and professional workers for courses, grades, or licenses. Attention must also be given to the applicants' ability to work with others on teams or with nontechnical managers. Behavioral-based interviews can be useful for that purpose. Ask questions like these:

- Tell me about a time when you were asked to work with a group that was not functioning as it should be. What did you do in the situation? How would you handle future situations like that?

- Tell me about a time when you were asked to convince people who lacked a technical background that you were right in your thinking. What did you do to convince them? How would you handle situations like that in the future?

It is also growing more important to assess applicants for their values and ethics. Technical and professional workers are not immune to the problems that have plagued other fields, such as financial institutions and, before that, to abuses involving Enron and other companies. Pose questions like these:

- Tell me about a situation in which you found yourself feeling uncomfortable professionally when someone asked you to do something you felt was wrong. Perhaps it had to do with manipulating technical results; perhaps it had to do with operating outside your own comfort zone in some way. What did you do in the situation? How would you handle future situations like that?

◆ Tell me about a time when you felt uncomfortable with the results of an analysis but had no more time, owing to a tight deadline, to carry out further analysis. How did you handle that situation? What would you do to handle situations like that in the future?

Additionally, recruiters of technical and professional workers can take steps to improve the ways their organizations look for talented people. Ten ideas are as follows:

1. Establish an employment brand that appeals especially to technical and professional workers. Become known for being worker-centered and for providing special challenges to new hires.

2. Train technical and professional workers how to talk about the organization when they are not at the company. Emphasize that what they tell other people will influence the quality of people who subsequently choose to apply. A bad employment brand will hurt the workers themselves by discouraging good people from applying. They will then have to handle more work.

3. Develop an onboarding program that gives equal weight to making people feel welcome and to becoming productive as quickly as possible.

4. Ask applicants to supply examples of their past work—and even ask college students to provide examples of what they regard as their best work. Interviews can be unduly influenced by appearance but work products are less likely to be regarded uncritically.

5. Encourage managers to refer qualified people they come across in social settings to consider applying for employment at the organization.

6. Encourage HiPros to become mentors for less experienced people by offering incentives.

7. Sponsor contests focused on technical problems for undergraduate and graduate students to solve, providing internships to those who succeed or contribute to solving these tough, real challenges that the organization faces.

8. Encourage managers and HiPros to teach part time at local universities and give them incentives for referring talented people to the organization.

9. Ensure that technical and professional applicants are interviewed by more than just the department manager, since one person may have biases that could be offset by other interviewers.

10. Train managers and others who do employment interviewing in effective interviewing techniques.

Use the checklist in Exhibit 3-3 to rate how well your organization is following these practices.

Creative Approaches for Recruiting Professional Workers

Research on recruitment has revealed that most employers use predictable approaches to sourcing new staff. These approaches include newspaper advertisements, search firms or employment agencies, campus recruiting, online and Web-based recruiting (sometimes called e-recruiting), radio and television advertisements, employee referrals, temporary agencies, and "help wanted" signs in or near the company. Employers should, of course, keep track of which approaches yield the most applicants, as well as which approaches are least expensive and bring in the best people. Research suggests that the size of the employer makes a difference: small firms generally get the best results from employee referrals, while large firms often get the best results from online methods.

But if your organization does what every other firm does, nothing

(text continues on page 64)

EXHIBIT 3-3.

ASSESSMENT TOOL FOR RATING YOUR ORGANIZATION'S RECRUITMENT BEST PRACTICES.

Directions: For each best practice listed in the left column, indicate how well your organization is using the approach to recruit technical and professional talent. Scale: *0 = Not applicable; 1 = Not at all well; 2 = Somewhat well; 3 = Well;* and *4 = Very well.* Total the ratings and interpret your score based on ratings given below.

Recruitment Best Practices	How Well Is Your Organization Using This Approach?				
	Not Applicable	*Not at All Well*	*Somewhat Well*	*Well*	*Very Well*
	0	1	2	3	4
1. Establish an employment brand that appeals especially to technical and professional workers.	0	1	2	3	4
2. Train technical and professional workers how to talk about the organization when they are not at the company.	0	1	2	3	4
3. Devote time and attention to an onboarding program that gives equal weight to making people feel welcome and to becoming productive as quickly as possible.	0	1	2	3	4
4. Ask applicants to supply examples of their past work—and even ask college students to provide examples of what they regard as their best work.	0	1	2	3	4
5. Encourage managers to refer, for employment, qualified people they come across in social settings.	0	1	2	3	4
6. Encourage HiPros to become mentors for less experienced people by giving them incentives to do so.	0	1	2	3	4

	How Well Is Your Organization Using This Approach?				
	Not Applicable 0	Not at All Well 1	Somewhat Well 2	Well 3	Very Well 4
7. Fund competitions centered on technical challenges for under-graduate and graduate students, providing internships to those who succeed in solving—or contributing to solving—tough, real challenges that the organization faces.	0	1	2	3	4
8. Encourage managers and high professionals to teach part time at local universities and give incentives for referring talented people for employment.	0	1	2	3	4
9. Technical and professional applicants are interviewed by more than just the department manager, since one person may have biases that could be corrected by multiple interviewers.	0	1	2	3	4
10. Train managers and others who do employment interviewing on effective interviewing techniques.	0	1	2	3	4

Total

Scoring

37 to 40	Your organization is functioning effectively in recruiting technical and professional talent. Give your recruiting effort an A.
30 to 36	Your organization is doing B-level work in recruiting technical and professional talent.
18 to 29	Your organization is doing C-level work in recruiting technical and professional talent.
10 to 17	Your organization is doing D-level work in recruiting technical and professional talent.
9 and below	Your organization is failing in its attempts to recruit technical and professional talent. Work to improve it immediately!!

will make your firm stand out from the crowd. Your company will most likely lose out to more famous, high-profile firms that give applicants a future employment advantage when the company's name is added to the individual's resume. After all, what has more cachet—having worked for GE or having been at some organization that nobody has ever heard of?

For this reason, smaller firms must apply creative recruiting strategies if they are to be effective in obtaining outstanding technical and professional talent.[1] They must simply outsmart their larger, more famous competitors. They must make up for a lack of name recognition by excelling in other ways.

There are a few tricks of the recruiting trade that can be helpful in attracting technical and professional people. First, study the competing organizations and identify what they typically do. It is not possible to compete for talent unless you know what the competition is doing—or neglecting to do. Exactly *how* do they recruit?

Second, develop a profile of your ideal technical or professional employee. That profile will, of course, be different by occupation group. The ideal mechanical engineer will be different from the ideal civil, aeronautical, nuclear, or electrical engineer. Study the HiPros in the organization by group and discover what makes them so good. What makes them tick?

Third, find out where your organization's HiPros came from. Are there any patterns? For instance, did they come from the same schools? The same previous employers? The same previous supervisors or managers? Often there *are* patterns. You can seek more people from those sources by managing up the supply chain.

Fourth, find ways to get the jump on the competitors. Some employers look at technical and professional people only as vacancies occur. Let them, but that is shortsighted. An important goal of many recruiting efforts, as in talent management, is to slash the time it takes to fill positions with well-qualified people. That goal cannot be accomplished if you have to reestablish an image for an organization periodically as vacancies occur. A better approach is to maintain a constant presence in the technical talent marketplace so that you are ready when the need arises.

Fifth, get a jump on the competitors by targeting specific universities and by establishing close ties with them. Rather than dealing only with the placement office, ask to speak in classes, host summer jobs and internships, and develop close relations with professors who are likely to see burgeoning talent before those people reach the placement office.

Sixth, find approaches to drive traffic to your Web sites or other online vehicles for applications. Create chat rooms that bring together college students and current workers to discuss professional or technical challenges. Encourage workers to write blogs that describe some challenges they face on their jobs and how they are meeting those challenges. Prepare exciting YouTube videos, as Google and many other well-known firms have done, to make employment at the organization appear interesting.

Seventh, and finally, host a contest based on the real challenges that the organization is facing. Permit people to work on teams or individually to attack these real-world problems. Then, enlist senior technical or professional managers to review the submissions. The "winners" can receive a prize (such as a scholarship or internship) and may even be considered for full-time employment. The organization benefits by getting new ideas and the applicants are given real-world problems that develop their skills.

Selecting the Best Technical/Professional Workers

Employee selection has been the focus of much attention.[2] One trend today is to use more employment testing to find the candidates who are the most psychologically well adjusted and who possess the essential employment skills. Another trend is to substitute technologically based telecommunications methods—such as videoconferences—for expensive travel for interviews. Sometimes virtual tours are substituted for actual visits to an organization—again, in a bid to save money.

But sometimes low-tech methods are actually best. For instance, it is well known that "people tend to pick people like themselves." Men tend to be biased in favor of men; women are biased in favor of women; graduates of a school are biased in favor of graduates of the same school. The more that an applicant is a clone of the person making a selection decision, the more that he or she is regarded as an ideal candidate.

This "like me" bias can work against an organization, but it can also be made to work for an organization. If only one manager interviews a job applicant, then it is likely to work against the organization; managers are likely to clone themselves, and that does not work as competitive conditions change and the organization needs new people to face future, and perhaps unknown, challenges.

But if the organization asks several HiPros to interview applicants individually and it solicits individual reactions to those applicants based on their technical competencies, there is a good chance that the people who satisfy multiple HiPros will be high professionals themselves. It goes without saying that interviewers should, thus, be handpicked to ensure that they really are high professionals (as opposed to being their managers' favorite people) and should be trained to conduct competency-based interviews.

Onboarding the Technical and Professional Workers

Orientation is a program, but onboarding is a process.[3] When newly hired workers enter an organization, they are usually motivated to make a good impression. Wise employers try to anticipate what information the new hires will need just before they need it, and then they give it to them. For instance, before people arrive on the first day, they should know where to park and also should know their hours of work (when to show up) and where they are going (whom to report to). It helps also to give them the employer's handbook before the first day, advise them to read it, and maybe even tell them they will take a quiz on it!

Orientation should occur as quickly as possible on the first day. Workers should be systematically driven through the necessary paperwork and then given a briefing on the organization's strategy, current situation, and (as appropriate) existing technical or professional challenges. As they enter their departments and are released to their department managers, they should be given a twofold orientation to the department and its people. It helps to assign newcomers a coach or trainer and a peer mentor. Their roles are distinct: a *coach* or *trainer* ensures that the new hire becomes productive in record time; a *peer mentor* ensures that a newcomer feels welcome and is invited to participate in social events that include other workers.

On-the-job *onboarding* should be planned. Avoid the temptation to assign a new hire to an experienced worker, wave a dismissive hand, and ask the veteran to show the new hire "the ropes." Think out the order in which the new hire should be trained and reduce it to a checklist sequenced by what is important to learn—and also what knowledge should be transferred from the trainer and other experienced workers to the newcomer.

Recruiting and Selecting Workers to Replace Knowledge

It is one thing to recruit and select workers to do the jobs as described in the job descriptions. That has, of course, been the traditional approach to filling positions. Unfortunately, it leads to vacancy-by-vacancy thinking, without any regard for the comprehensive talent base of an organization or its divisions and departments.

But it is also possible to consider recruiting and selecting workers on the basis of their ability to do the job (as described on job descriptions), match the profile of adequate or outstanding performers or HiPros (as described by competency models), and replace the unique abilities of people whom the workers may replace. It does not have to be all-or-nothing thinking. But it does help if management sets priorities. Is it merely enough to get the job done in the short term? Is it necessary to ensure that the people chosen to do the work match the current or desired future talent profiles? And, of course, is it essential to replace some knowledge lost to the organization as people retire or otherwise leave? If the latter is the case, then it is necessary during exit interviews to list the unique talents or knowledge possessed by those individuals who are leaving. Are they regarded as high professionals? If so, what are they are particularly knowledgeable about, and is that knowledge something that can be replaced from inside or outside the organization through external recruitment, internal development, or a combination of them?

The point is that there is more to people's doing their jobs than their immediate performance. People have unique talents that can make them particularly productive or particularly gifted at what they do. Organizational leaders, while sometimes believing that nobody is irreplaceable, should also recognize that some people have unique talents and knowledge that others lack. That situation can and often should be considered when filling positions from inside or outside an organization.

Chapter Summary

This chapter addressed several important questions. First, what is a recruitment strategy, and why is it needed for technical and professional workers? Second, what is unique about recruiting and selecting technical and professional workers? Third, how can an organization build a powerful employment brand with technical and professional workers, and how is that done? Fourth, how should technical and professional workers be recruited and selected? Fifth, how should technical and professional workers be onboarded? And sixth, how can the recruitment and selection of workers also be a tool to replace invaluable knowledge?

4.

Developing Technical and Professional Workers

Preserving and leveraging the valuable knowledge of technical and professional workers requires a strong organizational commitment to employee development. It is critical to develop the talents of knowledge workers so that their contributions are informed and planned by the latest knowledge. People should be given opportunities to share ideas and learn from each other. Without a commitment to development, managers will not establish a climate in which workers are encouraged to pass on the knowledge they have gained from experience or create new knowledge through individual reflection or group interaction. In addition, because most of the knowledge worth transferring is gained from experience, managing the experience of technical and professional workers is critical to realizing their long-term potential.

What unique challenges exist for those intent on developing technical and professional workers? What are the starting points for launching a systematic approach to such development of technical and professional workers? How is a systematic approach carried out and then evaluated?

69

How can technical coaches help in this development, and what role should individuals play in their own development? How can development experiences be used to pass on and/or create valuable knowledge? This chapter addresses these important questions.

The Unique Challenges

There are several challenges unique to the development of technical and professional workers. First, technical and professional knowledge dates quickly; that means that workers face skill obsolescence unless their knowledge is updated constantly, and it is a special problem when individuals are hired for their specialized knowledge. According to one source, "half of what is known today was not known 10 years ago . . . the amount of knowledge in the world has doubled in the past 10 years and is doubling every 18 months."[1] Thus, learning how to learn is critical to job success as the way to avoid skill obsolescence. This requires competence in how to learn and a work climate that encourages real-time learning to solve problems and keep skills current.[2] But learning how to learn is not taught in schools, and the supportive work climate depends on what employers—and managers—do to encourage expansion of knowledge.

Second, employers face the threefold challenge of teaching technical and professional workers (1) what has been learned in the past based on experience, (2) what has been learned recently about meeting current challenges, and (3) what new developments in the field are on the horizon. That means that having a robust professional development program is critical if the potential for technical and professional workers is to be realized. Many such workers expect that kind of development and will leave the organization if they do not receive it.

Third, with technical and professional workers, it is important to combine technology-assisted methods (such as e-learning), social-networking methods (such as wikis, blogs, communities of practice, and social-networking sites), and opportunities for planned learning both on and off the job. Technical and professional workers are generally more tech-savvy than those in other occupations, thus they are more willing to rely on blended learning methods—and, indeed, often prefer it.[3]

Launching an Employee Development Program

Technical and professional workers deserve robust professional development programs because their knowledge becomes dated quickly and because their knowledge can be critical to the success of the business.[4] Launching a program for these workers requires an examination of technical and professional competencies.[5] Competencies, of course, describe the ideal performer and can be the foundation for technical career ladders.

What Elements Are Needed Most

The most important aspect of instituting a systematic approach to developing technical and professional workers is to secure management commitment to do it. Leaders at all levels must be convinced of the need for it. And they should be given regular updates about its progress so that they are aware of how these investments in development are paying off, financially or technically.

Almost as critical as having management commitment is establishing a program based on the profiles of ideal performers, both present and as needed in the future. A technical competency model is required for the groups targeted for systematic development. Without this competency model, the organization's leaders will not agree on what the business needs are and the development program will be subject to idiosyncratic, and sometimes capricious, preferences of individual managers.

The Technical Competency Models

There are three ways to develop the technical competencies that form the basis for the development program. The first is to "borrow" and immediately use a technical competency model from other sources. Some of these models can be found on the Web simply by going to a search engine and typing in "competencies" and then the name of the specialty area—such as "mechanical engineering" or "architecture." Other versions may be found by contacting technical or professional associations. Of course, using this approach has its disadvantages, since the quality of a competency study depends on how well it matches the corporate and national cultures where it will be used.

A second approach is to "buy and modify" a technical or professional competency model. Then the model can be tailored to fit the unique requirements of your corporate culture. That is a particularly popular approach, though finding these models is not as easy as locating them for management or for leadership. Exhibit 4-1 provides a list of Web sites to start your search. In many cases, professional associations will have technical competency models, too. These can be purchased and then adapted with less time or cost than building such models from scratch. For information on how to adapt such models, see Rothwell and Graber's *Competency-Based Training Basics.*[6]

A third approach is to build your own competency model. The made-from-scratch version uses behavioral event interviewing, posing critical-incident questions to job incumbents. They are asked to describe key challenges they have faced. (See an example of an interview guide for conducting behavioral event interviewing in Exhibit 4-2.) You then analyze the responses, looking for common themes, and determine measurable abilities based on behavioral indicators and/or work outputs. For information on how to analyze the themes arising from responses to the interview guide, see Rothwell and Graber's *Competency-Based Training Basics.*[7]

Once you have a competency model, you also have a basis for assessing individuals against a present and/or future competency profile. That assessment can be performed by managers or individual practitioners —or else through 360-degree methods. The resulting development gaps should be narrowed and made to correspond as closely as possible with

EXHIBIT 4-1.

SOURCES OF INFORMATION ON TECHNICAL OR FUNCTIONAL COMPETENCIES.

The Internet is helpful in locating sources of general information on technical or functional competencies, which can then be customized to fit your unique corporate culture. Here is a sampling of such sources.

Accountants

The American Institute of Certified Public Accountants; see http://www2 .gsu.edu/~acccws/ole/professional.htm.

Architects

See http://www.ask.com/bar?q=Architect+competencies&page=4&qsrc= 121&dm=all&ab=4&u=http%3A%2F%2Fwww.iasahome.org%2Fweb% 2Fhome%2Fcompetencies&sg=xrpB%2BdwdamQlvq%2BmYt2U5EHkw Dw1P0cbkoVGf%2BjVd1g%3D&tsp=1271539579833.

Bookkeepers

See http://www.eric.ed.gov/ERICWebPortal/custom/portlets/recordDetails/ detailmini.jsp?_nfpb=true&_&ERICExtSearch_SearchValue_0=ED282016& ERICExtSearch_SearchType_0=no&accno=ED282016.

Computer/IT Positions

There are many specialties, but these are a start. See An Investigation of Preparedness and Importance of MIS Competencies: Research in Progress, http://portal.acm.org/citation.cfm?id=1355260. For consultants, see Institute of Management Consultants USA, http://www.imcusa.org/?page= CONSULTINGCOMPETENCY. For researchers and R & D scientists, see Competency International, http://www.competencyinternational.com.

Designers

See www.id.iit.edu/141/getdocument.php?id=63. Also, see http://www.aiga .org/content.cfm/designer-of-2015-competencies.

Engineers

There are many specialties, but these are a start. For ABET competencies, see http://www.foundationcoalition.org/home/keycomponents/assessment_eval/ec_outcomes_summaries.html. Also, see Honor J. Passow, What Competencies Should Undergraduate Engineering Programs Emphasize? A Dilemma of Curricular Design that Practitioners' Opinions Can Inform, doctoral dissertation, University of Michigan, Ann Arbor, 2008; see http://deepblue.lib.umich.edu/bitstream/2027.42/60691/1/hpassow_1.pdf.

Veterinarians

Stakeholders weigh in on competencies needed by veterinary grads; see http://www.avma.org/onlnews/javma/apr10/100401a.asp.

the behaviors or work outputs that need improvement and the individual strengths that can be leveraged for the benefit of others. Needed development on behaviors or work outputs can then become the basis for action plans to guide professional development. The strengths are clues to what individuals can offer as mentors to others.

Implementing and Evaluating a Development Plan

Development is a broader term than *training.* Training is a short-term, individualized change effort designed to help people do their jobs. *Development* suggests a longer-term change effort designed to help individuals build their base of experience. About 90 percent of all development occurs on the job, as part of people doing their work.[8] The challenges given to people at work build their abilities to do better work through experience.

One way to think about the difference is to regard development as interwoven with work experiences.[9] People can be developed by *whom* they work for (the kind of supervisors they have), *whom* they work with (the kind of coworkers they have), *who* works for them (the kind of

(text continues on page 79)

EXHIBIT 4-2.

INTERVIEW GUIDE FOR PINPOINTING TECHNICAL COMPETENCIES.

Directions: Be sure selected individuals ask only the questions provided and read the introductory statements as given in the study form below. Tape-record the responses, if possible.

Interview Guide for Behavioral Study Event

Your Name   Name of Individual Interviewed

_____

Respondent's Job Category

_____

Today's Date   Job Title of Individual Interviewed

_____

Employer of Individual Interviewed

_____

Background/Introduction

Thank you for agreeing to participant in this study.

How people manage work situations and work challenges is critical to their success. The purpose of this study is to identify the special competencies that workers need to succeed in this organization and in this job category or department. You will be asked about two major issues: the most difficult work situation you feel you have ever encountered in the workplace, and the most common or typical work situation you feel you encounter in the workplace. Please be detailed in your answers to the questions.

Respondent's Job Requirements

Question	Notes on the Answer
1. What are your work requirements? Tell me about your work duties.	*List work requirements and duties.*

(continues)

EXHIBIT 4-2. (continued)

Most Difficult Work Situation

Question	Notes on the Answer
1. Think back to the *single most difficult work situation* you have ever encountered in your job or in your department in this organization. This can involve any work activity or effort—so long as it occurred while you were in the workplace. It is important that you describe the situation in detail. First, provide an overview of the situation. What was the work challenge you faced? Then answer some background questions: When did this occur (approximate dates)? Who was involved (give job titles but not names)? Where did this occur (give approximate location)?	*What was the work challenge?* *When did this occur?* *Who was involved?* *Where did this occur?*

	Step by Step	What was happening and what were you doing?	What were you thinking as this was happening and/or as you were doing what you were doing?	What were you feeling as this was happening and/or as you were doing what you were doing?
2. Tell us how you performed in this situation. Be as specific as possible, describing what happened in the sequence that it happened. Be sure to explain what was happening, what you were doing, what you were thinking, and what you were feeling as events unfolded.	1			
	2			
	3			
	4			
	5			
	6			
	7			
	8			

Question	Notes on the Answer
3. What did you learn about how you should perform in situations like this? If you faced the same situation again, how would you handle it—and why would you handle it that way?	*What did you learn about how you should perform in situations like this?* *If you faced the same situation again, how would you handle it?* *If you faced the same situation again, why would you handle it the way you said you would handle it?*

Most Common or Typical Challenging Work Situation

Question	Notes on the Answer
1. Think about the *most common or typical work challenge* you encounter in the workplace. This can involve *any* work activity or effort—so long as it occurs while you are in the workplace. First, provide an overview of the situation. What is the typical work challenge you face? Then answer some background questions: When does this occur? Who is involved? How often does it occur? Why do you think it occurs?	*What is the typical work challenge?* *When does this occur?* *Who is involved?* *How often does it occur?* *Why do you think it occurs?*

	Step by Step	*What was happening and what were you doing?*	*What were you thinking as this was happening and/or as you were doing what you were doing?*	*What were you feeling as this was happening and/or as you were doing what you were doing?*
2. Tell us how you handle this situation. Be as specific as possible, describing what happens in the sequence that it happens. Be sure to explain what is happening, what you are doing, what you are thinking, and what you are feeling as events unfolded.	1			

continues)

EXHIBIT 4-2. (continued)

Step by Step	What was happening and what were you doing?	What were you thinking as this was happening and/or as you were doing what you were doing?	What were you feeling as this was happening and/or as you were doing what you were doing?
2			
3			
4			
5			
6			
7			
8			

Question	Notes on the Answer
3. What have you learned about how you should manage or handle this most common or typical work challenge? If you were advising others how to approach the situation, what advice would you give them and why?	What have you learned about how you should handle this most common or typical challenging work situation?
	If you were advising others how to approach the situation, what advice would you give them?
	Why would you give others the advice that you would give them?

Thank You for Your Cooperation!

workers they are given to supervise), *whom* they serve (the kind of customers they are to satisfy), what work challenges they are given (start an operation; shut down an operation; turn around a failing operation; apply a new technology), *what* they learn by accident as a result of what they do, *what technology* they are given to work with, *what time pressures* they face (working under pressure), *where* they are assigned (functional areas and geographical locations), and *how* they work (line or staff). Try brainstorming, just for practice, a list of work experiences that develops each behavioral indicator (or work output) of one competency, using the worksheet in Exhibit 4-3.

Individual Development Plans as Basis for Development

It is possible, and also desirable, to *plan* for each competency and each behavior linked to the competency that individuals are to develop. That planning should be done on an individual development plan (IDP), prepared at least annually and negotiated between workers and their immediate supervisors. An IDP is the action plan to guide each worker's development. When many workers share the same need, it is cost-effective to launch group efforts to meet the need. But when only one worker has a need, he or she should carry out appropriate competency-building activities on or off the job.

The IDP can also focus on what knowledge individuals should transfer to others, or how experienced workers should mentor others in areas in which they are particularly good or gifted. By using IDPs for that purpose, the organization's leaders can then begin to target what knowledge to transfer, how to do it, and who will do it. That is, it is a way to implement knowledge transfer, as well as to build technical competencies. Sample IDPs can be found easily on the Web simply by going to a search engine and entering the term "individual development plan."

Action Learning

In recent years, action learning has emerged as an important approach to worker development.[10] Sometimes called the "goal-based scenario," ac-

EXHIBIT 4-3.

WORKSHEET FOR BRAINSTORMING SESSION ON WORK EXPERIENCES TO DEVELOP COMPETENCIES AND THEIR BEHAVIORAL INDICATORS.

Directions: Assemble a group of managers and use this worksheet to brainstorm a list of work experiences—that is, on-the-job experiences—that would help individuals develop technical competencies; alongside, list each behavioral indicator of that competency. In column 3, list ways that the individuals can build their competencies and improve their behaviors.

	Technical Competency	Behavioral Indicator	How Many Ways Could This Behavioral Indicator Be Developed?
1	*Example*: Blueprint preparation	*Example*: Prepares blueprints using appropriate software	
2			
3			
4			
5			
6			
7			
8			

tion learning involves giving worker teams a real problem to solve, with a threefold demand to solve the problem, develop the team's individuals by giving them experience, and facilitate cross-functional development. A team leader is elected or appointed to ensure that the task is accomplished, and a facilitator is assigned to be sure there is the highest possible interpersonal involvement of team members in reaching the solution. Group members are briefed about the problem and are given limited time, money, and expertise; working together, they attack the problem and experiment with possible solutions, which provide an outlet for innovation. When the team reaches a limitation—runs out of time or money—or finds an acceptable solution, the group is disbanded. At that point, team members are debriefed individually and collectively about what they have learned, how they should develop in the future, and how they worked together as a team.

Action learning has the appeal of being based in the real world. Unlike off-the-job classroom settings, workers face real-world consequences for failure. They are also less likely to experience what is termed the *transfer of learning problem* that is so common with off-the-job training. Only 8 percent of off-the-job training transfers back to a job with changed behavior, largely because of short-term memory loss—about 80 percent of everything a human being hears is forgotten within 48 hours—and lack of support from peers or supervisors back on the job. In contrast, action learning encourages cross-functional development, giving technical and professional workers exposure to other parts of the business, as well.

The competencies that action learning can develop depend, of course, on the problem that a team is tasked to solve. For example, if individuals share a need to learn more about budgets and thereby build their budgeting skills, the task force can identify existing problems with the company's budgeting methods and come up with ways to solve them. That necessarily requires them to become familiar with the budget—and go a step further to improve it. The same idea can be applied to technical problems. For instance, an engineer can work on a project with a more experienced professional peer to learn firsthand how to solve problems inherent to such a project.

Unlike training, which may give participants limited exposure and thus restrict the consequences of poor participation, action learning requires the learners to take visible action. Individuals who do not participate are likely to stand out; and the consequences of not taking action become greater. Learners simply have to exert themselves more; they face real-world consequences for not doing so.

Best Practices in Developing Technical/ Professional Workers

An organization can take steps to develop its technical and professional workers. Several ideas for development include:

- Establishing measurable professional-development goals for each worker annually

- Aligning professional development to the organization's strategic objectives

- Aligning professional development to the individual's career objectives

- Clarifying the role to be played by the individual and the manager in professional development

- Establishing accountabilities for professional development for individuals and their managers

- Encouraging individuals to identify and develop their greatest technical or professional strengths, as well as work to overcome their weaknesses

- Establishing technical and functional competencies as a foundation for development

- Encouraging on-the-job development of competencies through work assignments, coaching, mentoring, and many other practical, real-time approaches

- Encouraging development through social networking and peer relationships

- Providing the time, money, and support essential to build competencies through off-the-job experiences inside or outside the organization

Use the checklist in Exhibit 4-4 to rate your organization's attempts to adhere to these practices. You may also use it to reflect on how your organization can improve its professional development in specific areas.

Using Technical Coaches

A *technical coach* is someone who guides others to do their technical work more effectively. In theory, anyone with more experience than the people they set out to help can be a technical coach. But that does not mean that everyone wants to play the role—or has the coaching competency to do so. Technical coaches may carry out their role in a job—some call centers have people with the job title *technical coach*.[11] Or technical coaching may occur more informally, as when peers give each other advice about how to solve a problem or when a manager gives his workers advice on solving a problem.

Coaching, in general, has been a popular topic in recent years. But technical coaching is somewhat different. To be effective technical coaches, individuals should:

- Master the basic skills of coaching, such as ability to establish rapport with others

- Demonstrate their credibility as people with sufficient experience with and knowledge of the subject

- Be able to reflect on what they have learned from their own experience—what to do and what not to do

- Be able to help people get started in solving a problem

- Direct attention to important matters that an experienced technical person will notice but less experienced people will not

- Emphasize what is worth knowing or learning, based on their own experience

EXHIBIT 4-4.

ASSESSMENT TOOL FOR COMPARING YOUR ORGANIZATION TO BEST PRACTICES IN DEVELOPING TECHNICAL AND PROFESSIONAL TALENT.

Directions: For each best practice listed in the left-hand column, indicate how well your organization uses the approach. Use this scale: *0 = Not applicable; 1 = Not at all well; 2 = Somewhat well; 3 = Well;* and *4 = Very well.* Add up your ratings and interpret the score using the scale given at the end.

	How Well Is Your Organization Using This Approach?				
Best Practices Approach in Developing Technical and Professional Talent	*Not Applicable*	*Not at All Well*	*Somewhat Well*	*Well*	*Very Well*
	0	*1*	*2*	*3*	*4*
1. Establish measurable professional development goals for each worker annually.	0	1	2	3	4
2. Align professional development to the organization's strategic objectives.	0	1	2	3	4
3. Align professional development to the individual's career objectives.	0	1	2	3	4
4. Clarify the role that should be played by the individual and the manager in professional development.	0	1	2	3	4
5. Establish accountabilities for professional development for individual and for his or her manager.	0	1	2	3	4
6. Encourage individuals to identify and develop their greatest technical or professional strengths as well as work to overcome their weaknesses.	0	1	2	3	4
7. Establish technical and functional competencies as a foundation for development.	0	1	2	3	4

	How Well Is Your Organization Using This Approach?				
	Not Applicable 0	Not at All Well 1	Somewhat Well 2	Well 3	Very Well 4
8. Encourage on-the-job development of competencies through work assignments, coaching, mentoring, and many other practical, real-time approaches.	0	1	2	3	4
9. Encourage development through social networking and peer relationships.	0	1	2	3	4
10. Provide the time, money, and support essential to build competencies through off-the-job experiences inside or outside the employing organization.	0	1	2	3	4

Total _____

Scoring

37 to 40	Your organization is functioning effectively in developing technical and professional talent. Give your development effort an A.
30 to 36	Your organization is doing B-level work in developing technical and professional talent.
18 to 29	Your organization is doing C-level work in developing technical and professional talent.
10 to 17	Your organization is doing D-level work in developing technical and professional talent.
9 and below	Your organization is failing to develop technical and professional talent. Work to improve it immediately!!

♦ Provide examples of how the technology has worked successfully in the past

♦ Let people try new methods on their own but watch them carefully

♦ Encourage people when they do something right and show ways they could improve when facing similar technical tasks

Use the tool appearing in Exhibit 4-5 to guide any technical coaching situations.

EXHIBIT 4-5.

COACHING GUIDE FOR TECHNICAL WORKERS.

Directions: For each task appearing in the left-hand column, indicate how you will accomplish it in the right-hand column. Use a fresh sheet for each occasion when you are coaching another person.

What Technical Coaches Should Do	*How Will You Do That?*
1. Master the basic skills of coaching such as establishing effective interpersonal rapport.	
2. Demonstrate their credibility as those with sufficient experience to be knowledgeable on the issues they are coaching about.	
3. Reflect on what they have learned from their own experience—what to do and what not to do.	
4. Help people get started in solving a problem.	
5. Direct attention to important issues that an experienced technical person will notice but perhaps less experienced people will not.	
6. Emphasize to those they coach what is worth knowing or learning about based on their own experience.	
7. Show people examples of how the technical work has been handled successfully in the past.	
8. Let people try to do it on their own but watch what the less experienced person does.	
9. Provide encouragement for what the worker did right and ways the worker could improve in the future when facing similar technical tasks.	

The Individual's Role in Development

The responsibility for professional development does not rest solely in the hands of a coach, a more experienced peer, or a supervisor. Individuals also have roles to play. The more active they are as learners—and the more willing they are to take the initiative to learn—the more they will benefit from development opportunities. It can even be helpful to train workers in what their responsibility should be in development.[12] Individuals should:

♦ Be motivated to learn and accept responsibility for taking an active role in the learning process by asking questions

♦ Reflect on their past experiences in learning situations to determine if they faced similar issues

♦ Take the initiative to start meeting the challenge

♦ Ask if there is anything special about the situation that the coach notices

♦ Watch what the coach does to solve the technical problem

♦ Try the solution on his or her own

♦ Ask for feedback on what was done well and what could be improved

Use the tool in Exhibit 4-6 to provide individuals with suggestions on how they can improve their performance as on-the-job learners.

Using Development Efforts to Pass on Knowledge

Developmental efforts can have purposes beyond building technical or professional competencies. They can also be a means for transferring valuable knowledge from those with experience to those who have not had

EXHIBIT 4-6.

LEARNING GUIDE FOR ON-THE-JOB TECHNICAL WORKERS.

Directions: Give this guide to all learners about to receive on-the-job training. For each item in the left–hand column, ask the learners how they plan to carry out the step. Review this list with them periodically to determine how effective their on-the-job learning has been.

What Should Technical On-the-Job Learners Do?	*How Will They Do That?*
1. Be motivated to learn and accept responsibility to take an active role in the learning process by asking questions.	
2. Reflect on their own past experience in learning situations to determine if they have previously had experience on the same or similar issues.	
3. Take initiative to get started in meeting the challenge.	
4. Ask if there is anything special about the situation that the coach notices.	
5. Watch what the coach does to solve the technical problem.	
6. Try it out on their own.	
7. Ask for feedback on what they did well and what they could improve.	

that experience and therefore have not acquired the specialized knowledge. But how is that done?

First, the knowledge transfer has to be planned. It may happen on its own, by accident, but it is always better to plan for desired results. Do that planning by posing explicit questions at the beginning of each learning event. For example, "What valuable knowledge can be transferred during the experience and/or the learning event?" Another is, "Who has had experience related to the issue or competency, and how can that be transferred?"

Second, recognize that not all knowledge possessed by those with experience can be easily articulated. Tacit knowledge is embedded in stories about that experience. For that reason, it is wise to encourage storytelling, focused on specific competencies or even behaviors or work outputs. Good methods to foster this storytelling are Friday pizza parties, online discussions, panel discussions with veteran performers, and brown bag lunches.

Chapter Summary

This chapter addressed several important questions:

1. What are the unique challenges involved with developing technical and professional workers?

2. What are the starting points for launching a systematic development program for technical and professional workers?

3. How is a systematic approach to worker development carried out and evaluated?

4. How can development efforts be used to pass on valuable knowledge?

5.

Retaining Technical and Professional Workers

As I tour the world, I hear a common complaint about the difficulty of retaining outstanding technical and professional workers. It is a persistent cry in the rapid-growth firms of the Asia-Pacific region; for example, I was told in Vietnam that the average turnover rate in many companies is 100 percent! When I asked how their HR departments manage to keep up with so much "churn," I was told that "they are part of the problem rather than part of the solution because they leave, too!"

Retention is an important part of any talent-management program. It is also an important part of any technical talent–management program. There are several important steps that decision makers can take to address a retention problem, and this chapter will describe them.

A related issue is the career paths of technical and professional workers, as these people are less likely to stay in organizations where they do not see a future. One way to build retention rates is to establish a *dual career ladder system*. One career ladder heads "up" the traditional organization chart, with increasing management responsibility. The other career ladder stretches "across" (sideways) a continuum of technical or professional expertise—sometimes involving broad and/or deeper exposure to the most specialized areas of the work.

What is the traditional definition of a career ladder? What is the basis of a career ladder? How are dual career ladder systems established? What are the advantages and disadvantages of dual career ladders as a means of encouraging HiPros to stay with the organization? What should be done to retain technical and professional workers? This chapter addresses these and other important issues.

Retaining Your Technical and Professional Workers

Organizations that wish to retain their technical and professional workers must take planned steps to do so. A typical problem at most organizations is that no organized effort is made to retain workers; HR professionals think it is the manager's job and the managers think it is HR's job. The result is that nobody does it. So, as a first step in solving a retention problem, decision makers need to develop a plan to address the matter and make clear what responsibilities each stakeholder group (manager, worker, and HR) has in retaining its people. Several ideas for retention include:

♦ Identifying HiPros who are worthy of retaining for what they know. Discuss them during talent review meetings, giving them equal emphasis as is often given to HiPos who are regarded as promotable. Indicate who the HiPros are, why they are worth retaining, what special knowledge each HiPro possesses, and what steps can be taken to transfer the invaluable knowledge to other workers.

♦ Setting targets for retention, realizing that very low turnover is not necessarily desirable, either. Monitor the turnover rates of HiPros. How many HiPros are in the organization, and how many are lost during different time periods? If *critical turnover* refers to the number of HiPos lost compared to the total number of HiPos, then *knowledge loss turnover* refers to the number of HiPros lost compared to the total number of HiPros.

♦ Recruiting for retention by seeking individuals who have reasons to remain in the area. Find out whether applicants have lived in the area before—and why they want to live in the area.

♦ Selecting for retention by examining the work history of applicants, looking for individuals who seem to stay with one employer for extended periods. Examine each applicant's work history, paying attention to how many jobs the person has held during different time periods. It is reasonable to conclude that people who jump from one job to another are likely to become turnover statistics. Try to find out why people quit and then consider that reason when deciding whether to hire a technical or professional person.

♦ Onboarding for retention by building a new hire's social ties to the organization. Encourage workers and managers to build social relationships with new hires by inviting them to events and other socializing. People are less likely to quit when they feel linked with the people they work with.

♦ Onboarding for retention by helping new hires become challenged by the work as quickly as possible. Periodically, ask them how challenged they feel—especially during the first six months—and then take steps to give them greater professional challenges if they signal the need for it. (Why six months? New hires are most likely to quit early on because their resumes are still floating among other employers; after six months, fewer employers will be competing for them.)

♦ Encouraging retention by investing in professional development beyond what is typical in the industry or in competing firms. Professional and technical workers usually judge employers by how much opportunity they provide for learning. Give them chances to learn and they will be reluctant to leave.

♦ Training managers in interpersonal skills so that they are more likely to treat people with respect and dignity, recognizing that most people "quit their bosses and not their jobs." When necessary, offer one-on-one coaching to managers to improve how well they interact with workers.

♦ Making retention a key performance indicator for managers. Track turnover rates by department and periodically display those statistics in meetings. That will encourage the managers to focus on retention, since no manager wants to top the list with a department that has the highest turnover rates of technical and professional workers.

♦ Finding out why people stay, and not just why people leave, so as to identify ways to intensify the intrinsic motivation individuals derive from the work. Ask the HiPros what motivates them most and what the organization can do to provide that motivation more often in the future.

♦ Modifying the exit interviews so that workers are asked what prompted them to seek alternative employment, rather than merely asking "Why are you leaving?" Workers will usually provide socially desirable reasons they are leaving, such as higher pay. But if asked what prompted them to look for alternative employment, different reasons may be given.

Use the checklist in Exhibit 5-1 to rate how well your organization is adhering to these best practices.

The Career Ladder as a Retention Tool

A *career ladder* is a way of describing an organization's promotion system. In most organizations, individuals are hired at entry level as *individual contributors,* meaning that they do not manage other people. As they acquire more knowledge, skill, and experience, the individual contributors may be considered for promotion to supervisor of a group of individual

EXHIBIT 5-1.

ASSESSMENT TOOL FOR YOUR ORGANIZATION'S USE OF BEST PRACTICES FOR RETAINING TECHNICAL AND PROFESSIONAL TALENT.

Directions: For each best practice listed in the left-hand column, indicate how well your organization is using the approach. Use this scale: *0 = Not applicable; 1 = Not at all well; 2 = Somewhat well; 3 = Well;* and *4 = Very well.* Add up your ratings and interpret your score according to the scale at the end.

Best Practices Approach in Retaining Technical and Professional Talent	How Well Is Your Organization Using This Approach?				
	Not Applicable	*Not at All Well*	*Somewhat Well*	*Well*	*Very Well*
	0	*1*	*2*	*3*	*4*
1. Set targets for retention, realizing that very low turnover is not necessarily desirable.	0	1	2	3	4
2. Identify High Professionals (HiPros) who are worthy of retaining for what they know.	0	1	2	3	4
3. Recruit for retention by seeking individuals who have reasons to remain in the area.	0	1	2	3	4
4. Select for retention by examining the work history of applicants, looking for individuals who seem to stay with one employer for extended periods.	0	1	2	3	4
5. Onboard for retention by building social ties to the organization.	0	1	2	3	4
6. Onboard for retention by helping individuals become challenged by the work as quickly as possible.	0	1	2	3	4
7. Encourage retention by investing in professional development beyond what is typical in the industry or in competing firms.	0	1	2	3	4

	How Well Is Your Organization Using This Approach?				
	Not Applicable	Not at All Well	Somewhat Well	Well	Very Well
	0	1	2	3	4
8. Train managers in interpersonal skills so that they are more likely to treat people well, recognizing that most people "quit their bosses and not their jobs."	0	1	2	3	4
9. Make retention a key performance indicator for managers.	0	1	2	3	4
10. Find out why people stay, and not just why people leave, so as to find ways to intensify the intrinsic motivation individuals derive from doing the work.	0	1	2	3	4

Total

Scoring

37 to 40	Your organization is functioning effectively in retaining technical and professional talent. Give your retention effort an A.
30 to 36	Your organization is doing B-level work in retaining technical and professional talent.
18 to 29	Your organization is doing C-level work in retaining technical and professional talent.
10 to 17	Your organization is doing D-level work in retaining technical and professional talent.
9 and below	Your organization is failing to retain technical and professional talent. Work to improve it immediately!!

contributors or as a team leader within a project-oriented organizational structure. Further advancement may require additional progress upward on the organization ladder, or chart.

One classic problem with the traditional career ladder is that the number of possible promotions decreases at each successively higher level on the organization's chain of command.[1] There are simply fewer supervisors and team leaders than individual contributors, fewer middle managers than front-line supervisors or team leaders, and fewer executives than middle managers. That leads to intense competition among workers for an ever-dwindling number of promotions up the ladder. It may also encourage highly talented people, who see little opportunity to enhance their income through promotion, to seek opportunities in other organizations.

To make matters worse (from the perspective of workers), organizations in the last twenty years have been *delayering*. This means that reorganization has reduced the number of management-level positions available. As a consequence, the number of people reporting to any one manager is increased.

One of the reasons for delayering is to increase the speed of decision making by reducing the number of layers through which a decision must pass for approval. Additionally, delayering improves communication from top to bottom of the organization by reducing the number of filtering layers that block information flow. Of course, delayering also has the unfortunate side effect of reducing the number of management positions. But it does cut the organization's management costs.

The Types of Career Ladders

Career ladders can be based on time on the job, job descriptions, the qualifications found in job specifications, the technical competencies of a given specialty area, or some combination of these factors.[2] The easiest career ladders to develop are those based on time. That is, individuals are given prearranged "promotions" (or at least movements on a predetermined salary schedule) as they reach specific milestones for time in their jobs. These are easiest to measure simply because tracking time is recordable. Of course, time on the job or with the organization may have little or nothing to do with productivity or professional contributions.

Career ladders may also be based on educational achievement. That is, the more education an individual receives, the higher up the ladder, with promotions given to acknowledge the value of higher education. It is also easy to count degrees earned, but, of course, educational attainment may have little or nothing to do with productivity or professional contributions.

Career ladders may be based on job difficulty. To do so requires detailed descriptions of the work performed at every level of the organization. Unfortunately, traditional job descriptions, while helpful, are usually not detailed enough to provide career guidance. But more detailed analysis, using approaches such as the developing a curriculum (DACUM) method, can be most helpful in identifying specific work challenges. Individuals can be assessed based on what they can and cannot do, and a continuum can be devised founded on the relative challenge of the work performed.

Career ladders may also be based on technical competencies. A technical competency model describes the ideal performer at each level of the organization, acquired by making a detailed examination of successful and/or superlative performers so as to pinpoint the characteristics they share that lead to the ability to get results. Technical competency models may also make it possible to pinpoint individuals who possess unique expertise because they are exemplary ("best in class") in *one* competency area.

Dual Career Ladders

Dual career ladders are usually developed in two major ways. The first, and the oldest, is called the *descriptive approach.* Its basis is an examination of the common elements in the career paths of individuals who have been promoted over an extended time span. Their careers are examined to see how they progressed from bottom to top, and they are interviewed to learn what they believe are the key points they learned at each rung (job) of the ladder. They are also asked what preparation they lacked, so that some form of preparation can be provided to other individuals to make up for perceived deficiencies.

An advantage of this first approach is that it is based on real people and real career paths. The credibility of the approach is unassailable, since the individuals who were interviewed can be identified. Doubters can always be shown case examples so that they may hear for themselves what these people believe. But a disadvantage of this approach is that it is not based on the ideal but is instead based on business expediency. Individuals are promoted up a career ladder so as to manage people, but that does not necessarily include meeting increasing technical challenges.

The second method, and more recent than the first, is called the *prescriptive approach.* It is based on the technical competencies of the functional area in which a worker is placed, such as marketing, engineering, or IT. No individuals are examined, but the technical competencies are arranged in a hierarchy, usually by expert panels facilitated by consultants or an organization's internal HR staff. Then the hierarchies are examined for exemplary performers—the HiPros who are best in class for their competencies. These individuals provide suggestions on how to arrange the competencies, behavioral indicators, and/or work outputs and they recommend specific developmental approaches individuals can take to build their technical or professional competence.

An advantage of this second approach is that it is based on logical relationships among the technical competencies, guided in part by the wisdom of best-in-class performers. But a disadvantage is that it is not based on reality but is instead based on expert advice. That advice may, or may not, be informed by the needs of the business. Professionals in any field often have a tendency to go overboard in their zeal for challenge. The level of expertise they need may have less to do with business needs and more with their ardor in learning all they can about their chosen field. While encouraging that ardor will usually also encourage retention, it may not always produce practical results for the business.

Dual Career Ladders, in Practice and Theory

Dual career ladders are desirable in theory but are not always practical. One reason is that HR professionals, charged with administering the dual career ladders, do not always understand the intricacies of the technical fields. And, in any case, they are steeped in a tradition that prizes vertical promotion over horizontal. Finally, if a genuine goal of management is to cut costs rather than to attract, develop, and retain the best and brightest people, then the costs of implementing a dual career ladder may be too high.

In fact, in the real world, organizations that have tried to establish dual career ladders have often failed to do so. One reason is that management ties pay to promotions and links promotions to practical knowledge acquired. But in almost every case, managers underestimate how much people will develop themselves when given the incentive to do so. In one actual case—at a hospital—nurses were told they would be granted "professional promotions" along a continuum from "Nurse I" to "Nurse XII" based on points accumulated by rotating among different departments, taking more training or obtaining additional professional education, or having other developmental experiences (such as participating on committees of professional associations). Management budgeted 5 percent in salary increases for these "horizontal" promotions. But the nurses were so motivated that the 5 percent fund was exhausted within one month, and management indicated that they would no longer reward such development. The result was that turnover skyrocketed, and the workers lost all trust in the hospital's management.

The Advantages and Disadvantages of Dual Ladders

Provided that the difficulties of designing and administering a dual career ladder can be overcome, an organization choosing to do so realizes some distinct benefits. For example, workers can see the advantages both to improving their technical and/or professional ability and to obtaining vertical advancement. In short, they have two ways—not just one—by which to obtain promotions. That appeals to those who may seek higher income and have no preferences whether they manage others or develop their technical expertise. And, for the organization, it may encourage people to develop their ability to both manage others and deepen and broaden their technical expertise.

Another benefit to a dual career ladder system is that it has strong appeal in recruiting. Likewise, the dual career ladder encourages people to stay with the organization longer, thus increasing retention.

But how about the disadvantages of having a dual career ladder? It is one thing for managers to say "let's have dual career ladders" and quite another to make them work—or make them workable. In a blog "Dual Career Ladders," authors Ted Leung and Jim Robertson do a masterful job of portraying the perils of dual career ladders as they exist in many high-tech firms today.

> The personnel system of a large corporation is designed to both motivate and control employees. . . . Promotions come quickly at first and are based as much on time-in-grade as accomplishments. Although there are some exceptions, neither accomplishments nor foul-ups have much effect on a person's advancement. Advancing still higher on the ladder becomes increasingly difficult, because the higher someone gets on the ladder, the more expensive they are in terms of both salary and benefits, and the fewer the number of people needed at those levels. Only the few who can demonstrate both their technical ability and their ability to get things done are promoted to the highest rungs.
>
> Many high-tech companies maintain what are called "dual career ladders." The idea is that talented technical people shouldn't feel that they have to take management jobs in order to advance in their careers; that they can advance through the excellence of their technical work. So early in an employee's career, a branching point is reached, and a person chooses (or is chosen for) either the managerial ladder or the technical ladder. The titles are different in each ladder, but pay and prerequisites are supposed to be the same, rung for rung. Of course, the managerial ladder extends into the executive ranks, while the technical ladder stops far short of this. This makes the managerial ladder appear more desirable to ambitious young employees.
>
> In theory, people can switch back and forth between the managerial and technical ladders. This is actually quite a good career strategy, because it gives an employee managerial experience while allowing him or her to remain technically competent.

Unfortunately, switching between ladders is difficult and not done by very many employees.

People who go into management are generally not technical whiz kids. Technical work is something they want to get out of as quickly as possible. It's difficult and not as satisfying to them as working with people. So they go into management and work hard to stay there, fighting for ever larger and more prestigious projects to manage since this is their entree into the ranks of higher management. In short order, however, overwhelmed by their managerial duties, it becomes impossible for them to maintain, never mind develop, technical competence, which they are mostly not interested in anyway.

On the technical side, the picture is equally grim. On this ladder, people are encouraged to focus deeply, become experts on one or more aspects of technology, and take leadership roles in developing emerging technologies. Many people do this well, but have a devil of a time getting anyone on the management side to listen to them. The problem is that the techies have a hard time navigating the maze—they haven't been trained. And the higher up the technical ladder they are, the worse it gets. Eventually, they get put into advanced technology or advanced design departments where they can be used as occasional consultants or safely ignored.[3]

Chapter Summary

This chapter addressed several important questions. First, what is the traditional definition of a career ladder? Second, what is the basis of a career ladder? Third, how are dual career ladder systems established? Fourth, what are the advantages and disadvantages of dual career ladders as a means of encouraging high professionals to stay with the organization? Fifth, and finally, what should be done to retain technical and professional workers?

6.

Managing and Engaging Technical and Professional Workers

Managing technical and professional workers can be especially challenging, some believe. As Bernard Rosenbaum wrote some years ago:

> Leaders of scientists and engineers must be able to understand and respond to the special needs of technical professionals. Such needs include a desire for autonomy and achievement. Technical professionals tend to identify primarily with their profession and secondarily with their company. Further, they are more resistant to internalizing and committing to mandated organizational goals than are most occupational groups. Given the strong characteristics of technical professionals, managing them requires special knowledge, strategies, and tactics. The technical professional's need for autonomy, achievement, and personal growth is best realized when the structure of the job and the relationship with the manager promotes and supports self-management.

102

> Leadership activities that are crucial to this empowerment in-
> clude: 1. sharing information, 2. delegating responsibility, and 3.
> encouraging upward communication.[1]

Generally speaking, these workers are more educated than the average worker. They typically do not respond well to authoritarian, directive management styles, which are so common—whether or not admitted—in many organizations even today. Those who lead such workers need special competencies to engage and manage these people effectively. And those competencies should be demonstrated on a daily basis.

What unique challenges do many organizations face in managing technical and professional workers? What competencies are required from leaders of technical and professional workers? How are technical and professional workers "engaged," and how does an organization build an engagement culture for technical and professional workers? How is an engagement culture related to an innovation culture? What should managers do daily to build technical talent? This chapter addresses these questions and, by doing so, describes specific issues in managing and engaging technical and professional workers.

The Unique Challenges

There are several unique challenges involved in managing technical and professional workers, and these challenges plague many organizations. Indeed, they are the common source of many problems. And meeting these challenges can go a long way toward establishing a climate that engages the workers, reduces turnover, and encourages productivity and innovation.

Challenge 1: Choosing the Leaders of Technical/Professional Workers

A common mistake many organizations make is to promote technical and professional workers up the corporate ladder, based upon their job performance, technical skills or credentials, and loyalty to the firm. Many managers—and, indeed, many workers—assume that good performance in a job should be an important consideration in making decisions about promotions to higher levels.[2] While it is true that a promote-from-within policy does encourage people, and it usually leads to good worker morale, it is a fallacy to assume that success at one level will guarantee success at higher levels.[3] In short, good technical or professional workers—people with a solid grasp of their fields and the ability to deliver good results—do not always make good managers or leaders of technical or professional workers. There simply is more to it than that. To begin, managers and leaders of technical and professional workers need to have good interpersonal skills. Lack of these good interpersonal skills, including an appreciation of how people feel (what some call *emotional intelligence*), has led to many promotion mistakes.

A related problem is, of course, if the decision to promote is not based on past experience, how can decision makers know that a technical or professional worker will make a good manager or leader? After all, there is no way to observe how that person would function in that capacity. Does success as an individual contributor mean that an individual will be a good project leader? Not always. Does success as a project leader mean that an individual will be a good department head? Not always. There's more to picking people for higher-level responsibilities than leaping to conclusions, especially when there are no facts to support those conclusions.

One possible solution is to use *realistic job tryouts,* in which individuals temporarily assume responsibility for higher-level positions when their immediate supervisors are on vacation, out sick, or traveling to business meetings. Over time, these people's demonstrated ability to perform at a higher level is tested and thus their real development needs can be determined based on experience. While it is possible to use 360-degree assessments, assessment centers, or other approaches to assessing an individual's ability to perform at higher levels, none of these approaches is as effective as having him or her actually do the work and observing the performance.

Challenge 2: Training and Developing Managers of Technical/ Professional Workers

Another common mistake many organizations make is to assume that, to lead or manage technical or professional workers, all people need is the requisite technical or professional background. Often, the only credential required to manage medical doctors as hospital department head is a medical degree; the only credential required to be a department head in a university is a Ph.D. in the field; and the only credential required to manage salespersons is sales experience.[4] The same principle seems to dominate for many technical and professional jobs: The manager need only have suitable education and/or experience in the subject matter.

But is that all it takes? Of course, this is not to say that everyone should walk around with a business degree or an MBA; after all, nobody said that business degrees prepare people to manage other people. Indeed, business schools have often been criticized for inadequately preparing students to be future managers of human beings. The MBA curriculum prepares people to analyze data, not manage people.

So what is the solution? Many organizations take up the slack by formulating, implementing, and evaluating internal programs to teach managers, or aspiring managers, how to lead people. This is particularly important for managers of technical and professional people, for the simple reason that these workers often have a "people deficit."[5] That is, their interpersonal skills are not good. These special programs, therefore, address this "people deficit" with programs aimed at leaders of technical and professional people.[6] Similarly, some universities have established minors in leadership for technical or professional workers, so as to help students prepare to work effectively with others and improve their interpersonal skills.

Challenge 3: Maintaining the Quality of People Management

The quality of management in any part of any organization can, and does, have an impact on productivity and on turnover. Research on turnover repeatedly shows that the behavior of managers influences workers' decisions to leave.[7] Poor management behavior can also lead to disengaged workers, those who are not only unproductive but also so angry that they actively work to sabotage their employers. While managers may not be able to motivate people—motivation may come from within—it certainly is possible to "demotivate" people by treating them badly. How can that problem be solved? There are several ways, of course. One is to promote based, in part, on an individual's people skills. A second is to train managers on how to apply effective interpersonal competencies.

Leadership Competencies for Managing Technical/Professional Workers

The most effective managers of technical and professional workers make use of what might be called the *new essential skills.*[8] They are only new in the sense that, according to research, they have grown more important in recent years.

In addition to the requisite technical competencies and skills needed to give them credibility with those they oversee, technical managers should possess business acumen, advanced communication and interpersonal skills, critical thinking and problem-solving abilities, coaching and mentoring skills, capability of managing business change, and good financial management skills. It can be most useful to prepare managers of technical and professional workers by giving them training that develops these skills and any others that may be critical to achieving future business objectives. Management needs to provide aspiring or practicing managers with opportunities to learn the theories behind these skills and then to demonstrate their mastery of them. Hands-on practice, through role play and eventually on-the-job coaching, can be most effective in upgrading the quality of technical and professional management. That, in turn, can lead to solid results for the business.[9]

Engaging Your Technical and Professional Workers

The term *engagement*, in the sense of getting worker commitment, does not have an official definition. Nevertheless, it warrants discussion because it is an essential feature of managing technical and professional workers. To get a grasp of what engagement means in your organization, it can be useful to ask a group of managers to brainstorm what people are actually *doing* when they are fully engaged—and what they are *doing* when they are actively disengaged. From this view, you can then begin to build a culture within the organization that fosters engagement.

The Characteristics of Engagement

Most people agree that engaged workers feel an emotional bond to their organization and to their work. They are willing to recommend their organization to others as a good place to work and, in fact, they actively help the organization recruit good people with the right skills. They are motivated in what they do by more than mere money and are genuinely interested in, and even passionate about, what they gain from their work. They are also readily able to subscribe to what they perceive to be the values (what is good and bad) and ethics (what is right and wrong) of their employer.

A 2007 study by Gallup found that U.S. workplaces fully engage only 29 percent of their workers.[10] A majority of workers—54 percent—are not engaged. And, worst of all, 17 percent of workers are actively working to undermine the mission, objectives, and efforts of their organizations.

Technical and professional workers are a special case, of course. More often, they value professional challenge higher than anything else about their job.[11] Consider:

Henry Sauermann, an assistant professor of strategic management at Georgia Institute of Technology, and Wesley M. Cohen,
the Frederick C. Joerg Professor of Business Administration at
Duke University's Fuqua School of Business, analyzed survey data
from a sample of more than 11,000 scientists and engineers in a
variety of industries. Sauermann and Cohen reported their results
in an October 2008 National Bureau of Economic Research
working paper titled "What Makes Them Tick? Employee Mo-
tives and Firm Innovation." One of the topics the survey covered
was the importance the scientists and engineers placed on eight
different types of work benefits (salary, fringe benefits, job security, intellectual challenge, independence, opportunities for advancement, responsibility, and contribution to society). One key
finding: Among the survey respondents, rating intellectual challenge as a very important aspect of a job was associated with
spending more hours at work and with producing more patent
applications for a given effort level. In contrast, those who said
that job security was important to them tended to have lower-
than-expected patent applications.[12]

Hence, engaging technical and professional workers requires that attention be paid to building an intellectually challenging work climate.

The Construction of an Engagement Culture

Any attempt to build an engagement culture for technical and professional workers must go beyond the simple, step-by-step approach that
works for most employees in an organization. For these specialized workers, it requires that the organization's leaders see a need to build that
engagement and then take deliberate steps to do so. It is, in reality, an
organizational change effort that means altering the corporate culture
itself.[13] It does not happen overnight; rather, it requires a concerted effort,
sometimes over an extended time.

It may be helpful to launch the change effort by measuring important characteristics of engagement. Among them, the technical and professional workers:

- ◆ Say that they have an emotional bond to their organization
- ◆ Have an emotional bond to the work they do
- ◆ Will actively recruit others for their employers
- ◆ Tell other people good things about the organization
- ◆ Are genuinely challenged by their work
- ◆ Can point with pride to results achieved from their jobs
- ◆ Feel that their organization recognizes the value of their work
- ◆ Sense that their immediate supervisor treats them with respect and dignity
- ◆ Believe that their immediate supervisor encourages them
- ◆ Think that their immediate supervisor actively works to challenge them
- ◆ Subscribe to the values (what is good and bad) of their employer
- ◆ Adopt the ethics (what is right and wrong) of their employer

Use the assessment instrument in Exhibit 6-1 to help technical and professional workers measure their perceptions of their own engagement. If necessary, take further steps by using the interviewing guide in Exhibit 6-2 to identify what could be done to increase the engagement of technical and professional workers.

Integrating Innovation and Engagement

There is a difference between engaging workers and fostering a culture that inspires innovation. But research by the Gallup organization sup-

EXHIBIT 6-1.

MEASUREMENT OF TECHNICAL
WORKERS' ENGAGEMENT.

Directions: Distribute this questionnaire to your organization's technical and professional workers to measure how they perceive their level of engagement. For each statement in the left-hand column, ask respondents to indicate their *level of agreement* using this scale: *0 = Not applicable; 1 = Strongly disagree; 2 = Disagree; 3 = Somewhat disagree; 4 = Somewhat agree; 5 = Agree; 6 = Strongly agree.* There are no right or wrong answers per se, but collective analysis of responses can indicate generally how engaged these workers are. Add up your scores and interpret using the scale at the end.

How much do you agree with these statements?	Not Applicable	Strongly Disagree	Disagree	Somewhat Disagree	Somewhat Agree	Agree	Strongly Agree
	0	*1*	*2*	*3*	*4*	*5*	*6*
1. I have a strong emotional bond to this organization.	0	1	2	3	4	5	6
2. I have an emotional bond to the work I do.	0	1	2	3	4	5	6
3. I actively recruit for my employer.	0	1	2	3	4	5	6
4. I make it a point to tell other people good things about my employer.	0	1	2	3	4	5	6
5. I am genuinely challenged by the work I do.	0	1	2	3	4	5	6
6. I point with pride to results achieved from my job.	0	1	2	3	4	5	6
7. I feel that my organization recognizes the value of my work.	0	1	2	3	4	5	6

Level of Agreement

How much do you agree with these statements?	Level of Agreement						
	Not Applicable	Strongly Disagree	Disagree	Somewhat Disagree	Somewhat Agree	Agree	Strongly Agree
	0	1	2	3	4	5	6
8. I feel that my immediate supervisor treats me with respect and dignity.	0	1	2	3	4	5	6
9. I feel that my immediate supervisor encourages me.	0	1	2	3	4	5	6
10. I feel that my immediate supervisor actively works to challenge me.	0	1	2	3	4	5	6
11. I truly believe in the values (what is good and bad) of my employer.	0	1	2	3	4	5	6
12. I truly believe in the ethics (what is right and wrong) of my employer.	0	1	2	3	4	5	6
Total							

Scoring

61 to 72	Respondents are highly engaged in the organization. They can serve as role models for others.
49 to 60	Respondents are engaged in the organization, but there is some room for improvement in specific areas.
38 to 48	Respondents are engaged in the organization, but there is much room for improvement.
25 to 37	Respondents are marginally engaged and are probably looking for another job.
14 to 24	Respondents are slightly disengaged and are probably very actively seeking alternative employment.
0 to 13	Respondents are actively disengaged.

ports the notion that engaged workers are more likely to be innovative.[14] Managers can, and do, cultivate a climate and culture that encourages innovation,[15] widely recognized by many business authorities as a key factor in establishing and maintaining competitive advantage, at present and into the future.[16]

According to research on the competencies of managers who effectively inspire innovation, David Gliddon found that "the expert compe-

EXHIBIT 6-2.

INTERVIEW GUIDE FOR IDENTIFYING WAYS
TO INCREASE ENGAGEMENT.

Directions: Interview technical and professional workers individually or in focus groups, asking the following questions. Look for themes in the responses, then target those for action.

Individual or Group Interviewed   **Interviewer**

Today's Date   **Location of Interview**

What can the organization do to	*Responses*
1 Increase how much you feel emotionally bonded to this organization?	
2 Increase your emotional bond to the work that you do?	
3 Make you more willing to actively recruit talented people for jobs in this organization?	
4 Encourage you to emphasize good things you tell other people about this organization?	
5 Make you feel more challenged by the work you do?	
6 Encourage you to always point with pride to results achieved from your job?	
7 Consistently feel that this organization recognizes the value of your work?	
8 Consistently feel that your immediate supervisor always treats you with respect and dignity?	
9 Consistently feel that your immediate supervisor always encourages you?	
10 Consistently feel that your immediate supervisor always seeks to challenge you professionally?	
11 Help you feel greater connection to the values (what is good and bad) of the organization?	
12 Help you feel greater connection to the ethics (what is right and wrong) as demonstrated by the organization?	

tencies identified suggest a focus on the categories of (a) learning, (b) leading groups and teams, (c) motivation and energy level, and (d) management and delegation."[17] In short, to encourage innovation, these particularly good managers encourage people to learn, they effectively lead groups and teams, they demonstrate and motivate with a high level of energy, and they delegate tasks and responsibilities as a way to develop their workers. How those competencies are demonstrated may differ across corporate or national cultures, but they are worthy of attention when training, coaching, mentoring, and developing the managers of technical and professional workers. Use the worksheet in Exhibit 6-3 to structure your thinking of how those crucial competencies can be demonstrated in your organization.[18]

A Tactical Model to Build Technical Talent

While an effective TTM program cannot exist without a strategic framework to support it, individual managers can play a critical role, on a daily basis, in building a culture that encourages innovation and develops technical and professional talent. Without *tactical* (that is, daily) support, it is unlikely that a strategic TTM program will be implemented, let alone sustained. After all, 90 percent of individual development occurs on the job and is thus under the direct, daily guidance of an organization's managers.

It is worth emphasizing here that a strategic model is not enough to implement a TTM program. The strategic model may give the impression that senior leaders and HR are solely responsible for making it all work, but it is the technical and professional managers who attract, develop, and retain the talent, and who arrange to transfer their knowledge to other workers on a daily basis. Therefore, a tactical model is necessary as well. The tactical model clarifies what role that managers of technical and professional workers should play on a day-by-day basis to support the TTM program.[19] The tactical model establishes the accountabilities, role clarification, and key goals to be achieved.

EXHIBIT 6-3.

WORKSHEET TO DETERMINE WAYS MANAGEMENT CAN ENCOURAGE EMPLOYEES TO BE INNOVATIVE.

Directions: Use this sheet individually or with groups of selected managers in a brainstorming session. For each managerial competency listed in the left-hand column, indicate what observable behaviors managers need to show to inspire technical and professional workers to be more innovative. There are no right or wrong answers per se. However some answers may be better than others.

Manager Competencies That Inspire Workers to be Innovative	Observable Behaviors That will Inspire Workers to be More Innovative
1 Ability to encourage people to learn.	
2 Willingness to learn themselves.	
3 Effectively lead groups and teams.	
4 Demonstrate high levels of energy.	
5 Motivate other people to demonstrate high levels of energy.	
6 Know how to manage others.	
7 Teach or develop others through effective delegation.	

A tactical model to guide TTM is depicted in Exhibit 6-4 and is described below. Consider how well your organization's managers currently deal with TTM on a daily basis (see Appendix III).

Step 1: *Clarify the daily role of each manager.* Managers have a daily role—and a daily responsibility—to cultivate talent. And that is especially true of technical and professional talent. What is more, managers have a daily responsibility to ensure the transfer of valuable knowledge from those who have it to those who need it.

EXHIBIT 6-4.

TACTICAL MODEL TO GUIDE TTM.

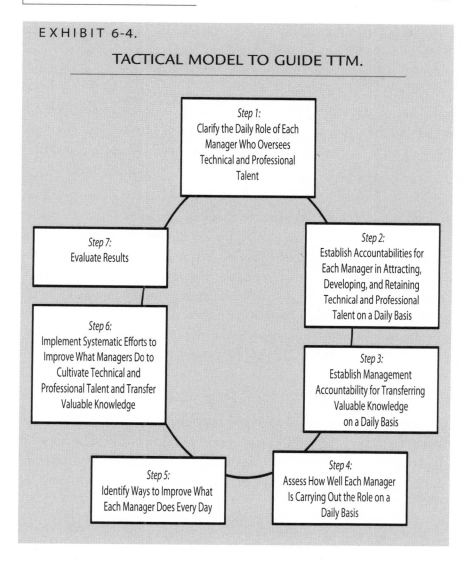

Step 2: *Establish accountabilities for attracting, developing, and retaining talent.* Each manager's specific accountabilities for attracting, developing and retaining talent should be made explicit. It should be added to job descriptions. It may also be added to each manager's key performance indicators. But it must be made clear.

Step 3: *Establish accountability for knowledge transfer.* Just as managers have the responsibility to attract, develop, and retain technical and professional talent, they also have the responsibility for ensuring the transfer of valuable knowledge from more experienced to less experienced workers. That responsibility should be made clear in the managers' job descriptions and in annual performance reviews. Specific targets should be established; the methods to be used are described in Chapters 7 and 8.

Step 4: *Assess manager performance.* It is difficult to improve managers' ability to attract, develop, and retain technical and professional talent if nobody knows how well they are doing it. The same principle applies to their ability to ensure transfer of valuable knowledge. Therefore, some effort should be made to establish targets and to measure periodically each manager's effectiveness so that the manager can be coached, counseled, and trained to improve this ability. An assessment could include asking questions on exit interviews of technical and professional workers (for departing employees) and on employee attitude surveys (to identify problem areas), both of which should encourage improvement efforts in this aspect of TTM.

Step 5: *Identify ways to improve performance.* Part of the TTM program should include ways to improve managers' ability to attract, develop, and retain technical and professional talent, depending on what the assessments of performance reveal. For instance, a task force of managers could identify possible new approaches that might work in different parts of the organization.

Step 6: *Implement systematic efforts to improve manager performance.* This additional step can take the form of special training. It may also include on-the-job observation and coaching. At the same time, managers who excel should be recognized and rewarded for their accomplishments in either attracting, developing, and retaining the technical and professional talent or in encouraging the transfer of technical information. For example, create a special recognition program for these managers.

Step 7: *Evaluate the results.* As premised here, the daily actions of managers have much to do with attracting, developing, and retaining HiPros. Their day-to-day actions also influence the willingness of their workers to transfer valuable knowledge. Consequently, the results of managers' daily efforts should be periodically evaluated against desired, and measurable, targets. In Step 4, targets for TTM for each manager are established; in this step, they are evaluated.

The important point here is that key stakeholders have roles to play in attracting, developing, and retaining talent. HR cannot, and should not be expected to, do it all. The divisional managers working directly with technical and professional talent need to be involved on a daily basis. If the above steps are not followed, then a critical element will be missing from efforts to improve the organization's technical talent management. For instance, one organization chose a simple way to improve the daily actions of its managers: each manager was given a daily calendar with one TTM idea they could do that day. Emphasis on the subject served to keep the idea of daily commitment to TTM on their minds—as well as providing practical ideas for how to do it.

Chapter Summary

This chapter addressed the following questions: What unique problems do many organizations face in managing technical and professional workers? What competencies are required from leaders of technical and professional workers? How are technical and professional workers "engaged," and how does an organization build an engagement culture for technical and professional workers? How is an engagement culture related to an innovation culture? What should managers do daily to build technical talent?

7.

Transferring Valuable Knowledge: Theory and Models

Of utmost concern to many technical and professional managers is the potential loss of institutional memory and proprietary knowledge as experienced workers exit the workforce owing to death, disability, resignation, or retirement. The most experienced workers are not just "warm bodies" or "pairs of hands" to do the work. They carry around in their heads critical, often proprietary, business information that has been gained from years of experience, as well as institutional memory set down while working in the same corporate culture for so many years. They "know the ropes"—and sometimes they even *invented* the ropes. When they leave an organization, both explicit and tacit (learned from experience) knowledge is apt to be lost. So, an important challenge many organizations face today is finding *practical* ways to transfer the knowledge of their most experienced workers to those less experienced.

But why is this knowledge transfer so important? What does *technical succession planning* mean, and what model can help to understand what it is? What elements are essential to technical succession planning? What practical approaches can be used to transfer technical and professional knowledge? What barriers exist to knowledge transfer that must be overcome to make a knowledge-transfer program work? This chapter addresses these questions.

Why Knowledge Transfer Is Important

Economists and historians trace the development of the modern world as moving from an agricultural basis to an industrial one. Today, some feel we have moved on to a third phrase. While the basic industries still exist, most present economic growth is spurred by information and innovation.[1] That has prompted such terms as "the information age" and, beyond that, "the innovation economy."

Human capital is today's key to economic growth and well-being. Talent, understood to mean the unique gifts an individual possesses, is essential to competitive advantage. Talent resides with people because machines, though helpful, cannot yet think, invent, or create. What people know and do—and how they apply their talents to achieve competitive advantage—is essential to the founding of companies, the creation of jobs, and the sustainment of both organizations and nations.

But human talent is a "wasting asset." It does not waste in the same way as fresh fruits, machines, or capital assets diminish in value, or waste away. But it wastes nevertheless because people die, become disabled, resign from their jobs, or retire from the workforce. When that happens, what they know and have learned from experience can be lost—unless organizations take steps to capture and transfer the knowledge of these people to others who can use that knowledge. And yet some research indicates that fewer than 40 percent of U.S. companies take any steps at all to capture and pass on what their most talented, experienced, and veteran performers have learned from experience. Of course, one way to preserve that knowledge is to keep it around—and that is exactly what some organizations do, by giving recent retirees short-term contracts, emergency callback arrangements, and other special deals to preserve their knowledge for the organization's benefit.

An Explanation of Technical Succession Planning

Say the words "succession planning" and you are likely to evoke an image in the minds of most managers and workers of steps to prepare the next generation of managers. The term *succession planning* is sometimes confused with *replacement planning,* the process of identifying short-term backups for key positions until a proper search for a qualified applicant can be undertaken. In many cases, succession planning is used to groom future leaders from within the organization.

But *technical succession planning* refers to the process of identifying critically important information about the organization's processes, customers, suppliers, distributors, or other elements of the work and passing it on to others.[2] While many people may confuse the term with the broader notion of *knowledge management,* technical succession planning is actually a subset of knowledge management that pinpoints the critically important information that is at risk of being lost and it seeks practical, useful ways to preserve and transfer it to others.

A Model for Technical Succession Planning

Technical succession planning is different from technical talent management, in that it focuses on developing internal talent and on transferring knowledge. Thus, the model for technical succession planning is different from that for TTM, the latter which includes attention to recruiting, selecting, developing, and retaining technical and professional workers. In many cases, organizational leaders begin with replacement planning, then gradually evolve that program to include technical succession planning and eventually technical talent management.

Whatever program is designed and rolled out, it helps to have a strategic model to guide the effort. A model facilitates discussions and decisions by managers at all levels, and can be used to explain the effort. Exhibit 7-1 is the model for technical succession planning, and it is described in detail as follows.

Step 1: *Clarify goals, roles, and accountabilities.* A technical succession planning program begins with commitment. Someone must see the need for such an effort and be willing to commit time, money, and staff to the effort. Note that it may not be necessary to launch the program at the top of the organization and roll it down; rather, a division director or department manager of a technical or professional unit could initiate it—provided the money, staff, and other resources are available. But it is important at the outset that you clarify why the program is being initiated (state measurable goals), designate the responsibilities of each manager to make the program successful (clarify key roles), and establish accountability methods to ensure the goals are achieved.

Step 2: *Identify key work processes.* A *work process* is any identifiable list of actions that lead to a result needed by the organization. For instance, all organizations purchase equipment, recruit and select workers, and deliver products or services to customers—these are work processes. But not all work processes are equally important. Given the organization's mission, certain work processes are critical to achieving that mission and to achieving its strategic goals on a regular basis. For instance, an automotive manufacturer would consider any process having to do directly with manufacturing as critical to the organization's mission. So, you need to make a list of all work processes directly related to the organization's mission. That task is easier if the organization has been pursuing process-improvement efforts to streamline its operations; in that event, most or all critical work processes should have already been identified.

Step 3: *Pinpoint the employees who possess specialized knowledge.* For each critical work process, identify (at least annually, so as to keep cur-

EXHIBIT 7-1.

MODEL TO GUIDE SUCCESSION PLANNING
FOR TECHNICAL WORKERS.

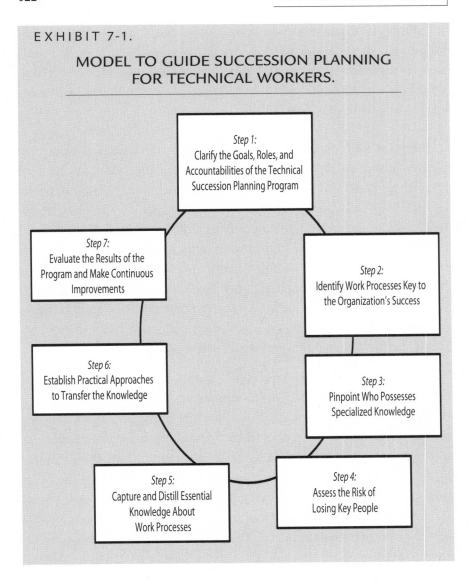

rent) the in-house experts. That is, who are the "go-to" people for each critical work process? What makes them the in-house experts? What special knowledge do they possess, and why is it important? Also include information about when the individual joined the organization, how long he or she has been in that position, what some of the individual's major work accomplishments have been, and other information that decision makers deem relevant to the organization. HR practitioners can be the keepers of the list—or else work with the MIS department to secure appropriate software for tracking this information. Such software does exist, and it is sometimes called "expert-finding software" (the term to use in doing a Web search for it).

Step 4: *Assess the risk of losing key people.* What loss will be experienced if the organization loses its key in-house experts? Consider such questions as these:

♦ How likely are these HiPros to leave the organization in the near future for any reason?

♦ What special knowledge do these HiPros possess?

♦ What will be the likely consequences if they leave?

♦ What risks will their loss pose to the organization?

One goal of such an assessment is to set priorities for capturing and preserving this vital knowledge. Remember, all knowledge is not equally important, but the loss of some expertise could be truly catastrophic. It is important to know what risks exist, what consequences may stem from them, and what should be done to capture that invaluable knowledge before it is lost.

Step 5: *Capture and distill essential knowledge.* Once you have identified the knowledge to capture and determined its priority, you can take steps to capture that knowledge from the HiPros and distill it for transmission to others.

There are many ways to capture the knowledge. It can be recorded by surveys, through interviews, in focus groups, and by observation. For example, it can be brainstormed and then distilled by a panel of HiPros or mapped to flowcharts, especially electronic flowcharts with mouseover links to coaching tips tied to specific steps in a work process.

Step 6: *Develop practical ways to transfer knowledge.* Some organizations have had bad experiences with knowledge-management programs. For instance, expensive software was purchased but was never used. So it is of particular importance to successful technical succession planning to find ways to transfer the valuable knowledge in practical ways—that is, in ways that people will use. People will not necessarily go to a computer-based knowledge-management system as their first step when seeking information. The next chapter discusses some practical ways to transfer knowledge; you may be able to think of others. But no matter what methods you use, pilot-test them first to make sure that they work. Corporate and national cultures differ, and what works at one place may not work in another.

Step 7: *Evaluate results and make continuous improvements.* The means for evaluation are always an issue, open to dispute. Measuring results is, and will continue to be, a major problem for technical succession planning. While there are various philosophies about what to measure and how to measure it, the best approach is probably to tie the evaluation process to the measurable goals initially established for the program. Alternatively, consider using a balanced scorecard aligned to the organization's measurable strategic objectives. In so doing, you can rate how well your organization has conducted its technical succession planning, using Exhibit 7-2.

Barriers to Overcome in Knowledge Transfer

There are some big barriers to overcome in successful knowledge transfer, some of which have been hinted at in previous chapters of this book. The

EXHIBIT 7-2.

TOOL FOR MEASURING EXTENT OF KNOWLEDGE TRANSFER.

Directions: For each item listed in the left-hand column, assess your organization's knowledge-transfer capability using the following scale: *0 = Not applicable to the needs of this organization; 1 = the organization does not do this effectively at all; (2) the organization effectively does this on occasion; (3) the organization does this adequately and regularly;* and *(4) the organization always does this effectively.* There are no right or wrong answers per se, as this tool measures perception, not reality. Total your score and then compare it with the rating that follows at the end.

	How Often Do You Believe Your Organization Adheres to the Characteristics of Effective Knowledge Transfer?					
Characteristics of Effective Knowledge Transfer	*Not applicable* 0	*Never does this* 1	*Sometimes does this* 2	*Regularly does this* 3	*Always does this* 4	*Notes or Comments*
1. Has clarified the goals, roles, and accountabilities of the knowledge-transfer program.	0	1	2	3	4	
2. Has identified work processes key to the organization's success.	0	1	2	3	4	
3. Has pinpointed who possesses specialized knowledge.	0	1	2	3	4	
4. Has assessed the risk of losing key people with specialized knowledge.	0	1	2	3	4	
5. Has captured and distilled essential knowledge about work processes.	0	1	2	3	4	
6. Has established practical approaches to transfer the knowledge.	0	1	2	3	4	

Characteristics of Effective Knowledge Transfer	How Often Do You Believe Your Organization Adheres to the Characteristics of Effective Knowledge Transfer?					Notes or Comments
	Not applicable 0	Never does this 1	Sometimes does this 2	Regularly does this 3	Always does this 4	
7. Has evaluated the results of the program and makes continuous improvements.	0	1	2	3	4	

Total

Scoring

26 to 28	Your organization appears to have an effective framework to support knowledge transfer.
23 to 25	Your organization has many elements of an effective framework to support knowledge transfer. Direct attention to the missing elements.
20 to 22	Your organization is not focusing attention on the potential, and perhaps disastrous, loss of knowledge. Do something!
0 to 19	Your organization is completely failing in its efforts to transfer knowledge.

first is management commitment, the second is obtaining truly valuable information, and the third is incentives to promote information sharing.

Management commitment is not an on/off switch; it is more like a rheostat. Many good knowledge-transfer efforts are undertaken to solve specific business problems, but without commitment they eventually fall short of expectation. Should a program be launched, there will be initial progress made in transferring expert knowledge, but there is now a danger that management will lose interest—and thus the program will fail. And so the real concern is how to sustain management commitment over time.

The second barrier is the difficulty of selecting practical approaches to knowledge transfer that will produce information people will actually use. Workers want real-time help. They do not necessarily think of going to procedure manuals or online databases as a first choice. The more natural thing to do is to approach other people, usually coworkers or an immediate supervisor. Hence, the hurdle is to find ways to overcome this unwillingness to change, to make it easy for people to access knowledge when it is needed.

The third barrier is the reluctance of the experts to share information. You have to make it worthwhile for HiPros to cooperate in providing their hard-earned knowledge. It is thus essential to consider how to answer the question "What's in it for me?" Those who possess information may regard it as their job insurance, their guarantee of job security. Of course, the most commonsense answer is to reward people, either financially or in other ways, for providing that information. A simple solution is employment contracts that give HiPros a sense of security. A second approach is to recognize their contributions; of course, that may also include financial rewards.

Chapter Summary

This chapter answered several important questions: (1) Why is knowledge transfer important? (2) Why is knowledge transfer so important in TTM that it deserves its own label as technical succession planning? (3) What model can aid in understanding technical succession planning? (4) What elements are essential in technical succession planning?

Knowledge transfer is important because it is increasingly the basis for an organization's competitive advantage. It is important enough that it may warrant special attention through a technical succession planning program. Technical succession planning identifies critically important information about the organization's work processes, customers, suppliers, distributors, or other critical matters, who possesses that information, and establishes a way to pass it on to others. This is a subset of knowledge management that pinpoints the information that, if lost, puts the organization at risk.

A technical succession planning program can be guided by a model that includes seven key steps:

1. Clarify the goals, roles, and accountabilities of the technical succession planning program.

2. Identify the work processes key to the organization's success.

3. Pinpoint those who possess specialized knowledge.

4. Assess the risk of losing key people.

5. Capture and distill the essential knowledge about work processes.

6. Establish practical approaches to transfer the knowledge.

7. Evaluate the results of the program and make continuous improvements.

8.

Transferring Valuable Knowledge: Practical Strategies

As suggested in Chapter 7, it is possible to purchase expensive knowledge-management software, hire a chief knowledge officer (CKO), and devote much time, money, and staff to building an elaborate knowledge-management system. It is even possible to find freeware and shareware on knowledge management.[1] But one lesson that many organizational leaders have learned is this: Elaborate, expensive, and complex systems rarely work as well as systems based on elegant simplicity.

Elegantly Simple but Effective

Elegantly simple systems for technical succession planning begin with one question in mind: *What will it take to formulate, implement, and evaluate a system to capture, distill, and transfer valuable knowledge with the least*

129

bother and the most likelihood of success? Consider the following approaches.[2]

Job Shadowing

A job-shadowing program is a simple way by which to transfer knowledge from one person or group to another. Typically, less-experienced performers are paired with veteran performers or HiPros. The veterans allow the less-experienced people to follow them around while they do their work. The veterans share their knowledge (and perhaps offer hands-on practice) in dealing with the most difficult situations they face on their jobs.

Some organizations have job-shadowing programs in which workers can identify specific people or positions they would like to shadow. The organization usually places a limit on the activity, such as one day of shadowing each year. A committee reviews the applications for shadowing and decides the pairings based on the organization's technical-talent transfer needs and priorities. Additionally, the HiPros are shadowed only when they agree to it—with a rule that prohibits certain people (such as the CEO) from being selected by everyone. Shadowing experiences can be split into two half-day components as well, allowing two different people to be shadowed by an individual in a single year.

One example of a job-shadowing program is that at AT&T. Its program is called ASPIRE and it is geared to students rather than to employees—indeed up to 100,000 students. AT&T pairs up the students with people in jobs they would like to get, thereby simultaneously offering a look at its employment opportunities .[3] Many universities (such as Notre Dame and the University of Toronto) and some secondary schools (such as career/technical education programs offered in many U.S. school districts) operate similar job-shadowing programs. But companies and other organizations can also offer job shadowing for their full-time staff as a means to transfer valuable knowledge.

Job Switching

One way to transfer knowledge is to encourage workers to switch jobs. Workers simply trade temporarily what jobs they do. That exchange can encourage cross-training and also prompt questions based on the different experiences encountered by each individual. Some organizations have established job switching programs with a view specifically toward encouraging knowledge transfer. One example is the North Carolina Office of State Personnel, where job switching is specifically recommended as one way to transfer knowledge.[4]

Job Rotation

Job rotation involves moving people to other jobs for a short or long time. It differs from job switching because the individuals know that the rotation is done only on a temporary basis and is usually associated with short-term movements while job switching may be for longer periods. Rotations may also be done part time (a few hours per week) or full time for an extended time (such as six months or up to two years). The rotations are undertaken with specific developmental objectives in mind for the employee. They can also be undertaken to encourage a less experienced worker to get closer to the HiPros for purposes of shadowing or informal knowledge transfer.

Communities of Practice

A *community of practice* is a group of workers that comes together to share information about a common problem, issue, or topic. Such communities meet in person, and others online. The meeting is a way to transmit knowledge from one person or group to another person or group, but also to store that knowledge. According to Wenger, McDermott, and Snyder,[5] specific actions enhance the formation of communities of practice.

First, the group should evolve naturally, out of common needs. Second, there should be encouragement of discussion within the community and also with groups outside the community. Third, different levels of participation will develop; some people will assume a leadership role, some others will participate actively but will eschew leadership positions; and some others yet will be loosely affiliated with the group (often the majority of people). Fourth, attention should be drawn to the value of the community and how people will meet their needs by participating in the community. Fifth, activities undertaken by the community should build excitement around the issues while maintaining familiar modes of interaction. Sixth, the group should assume a natural "rhythm" to meet, reflect on what they are learning, and evolve to higher levels of reflection.

Process Documentation

Popular as a result of ISO and the quality movement, *process documentation* involves flowcharting how an organization's work is performed. It may include special variations in what performers should do or show how they should do it based on special circumstances. Process documentation, which may include flowcharts and/or procedure manuals, is helpful in storing and transferring knowledge from more experienced to less experienced persons.

There are many ways in which to document work processes, of course, as well as to embed or situate knowledge from HiPros in the documentation. Software exists to facilitate how processes are documented and to encourage consistent ways to document processes.[6] What is important, however, is to ensure that some effort is made to capture the wisdom gained by in-house experts, based on their long experience. Make sure that their coaching tips are part of the documentation.

Critical Incident Interviews or Questionnaires

First described in the 1950s, the critical incident method takes its name from the tapping of lessons of experience. A *critical incident* is a difficult (critical) situation (incident). By documenting the experience gained and lessons learned by its HiPros, the organization can capture the fruits of their labor. Of course, by documenting such difficult cases and how they were handled, the organization is also laying the foundation for development of a procedures manual or automated expert system. Critical incidents provide an excellent basis for training.

One way to use the critical incident method is to administer it to HiPros. Ask them to answer the following question: "Tell me about the *most difficult situation* you ever faced in your job. What happened, step-by-step? Who was involved? When and where did this situation happen? What made the situation so difficult? What happened as a result of what you did? If you were to face the same situation again, how would you handle it and why?"

The critical incidents for all the HiPros are then analyzed for common themes.

Variations of the critical incident questions may be used. For instance:

1. Tell me about the *most common difficult situation* you face on a daily basis in your job in this organization. What happens, step-by-step? Who is usually involved? When and where does this situation usually happen? What makes these situations so difficult? What happens as a result of what you do? What have you learned from experience about what to do in these situations? What advice would you give others who face these situations?

2. Tell me about the *most exciting, energizing, and motivating situation* you have ever faced on your job in this organization. What happened step-by-step? Who was involved? When and where did this situation happen? What made the situation so exciting to you? What happened as a result of what you did? How do you think the organization could give you this feeling more often while still getting the work done?

3. Tell me about the *most exciting, energizing, and motivating situation* you face on your job in this organization nearly every day. What happens step-by-step? Who is usually involved? When and where does this situation usually happen? What makes these situations so motivating? What happens as a result of what you do? What have you learned from experience about what to do in these situations?

The critical incidents identified in each case can almost immediately be turned into training activities with a view toward transferring valuable knowledge (see Exhibit 8-1).

Job Aids

A *job aid* is anything that helps people perform in real time (that is, at the exact moment needed). A checklist is one example of a job aid. Checking off items on a list ensures that all steps are followed in a process. But checklists and other job aids like them are a means also for storing knowledge that can be accessed through low-tech methods when the need arises. While job aids have their limitations—it is not wise, for instance, to use a checklist when performing a medical operation because doing so undermines the credibility of the doctor—they can be useful in transferring knowledge from experts to others.

Many job aids exist, and each can serve to usefully transfer knowledge. See the extensive literature on job aids to determine how many options your organization has to transfer knowledge in real time.[7]

Storyboards

A *storyboard* is literally a series of pictures that tell a story. Think of a set of pictures placed on a wall or a poster that is intended to show how someone should perform a procedure in a specific situation, and you get the idea. For instance, posters in restaurants show someone how to perform the Heimlich maneuver, should a choking emergency arise. Airplanes show the procedures for removing the emergency doors in the

EXHIBIT 8-1.

TRAINING ACTIVITY BASED ON CRITICAL INCIDENTS.

Directions: Divide a group of workers into teams of two. For each critical incident listed in the left-hand column, have them come up with what they would do in the situation. After they complete the activity, provide information about how the individual who faced the situation handled it.

Critical Incident	*What Your Team Would Do and Why*
1. *Insert critical incident information here directly from what is collected from the critical incidents gathered from people in the organization*	
2.	
3.	
4.	
5.	
6.	
7.	
8.	

event of an accident. These picture series can also be an effective way to transfer knowledge, guaranteeing consistency and thoroughness.

Graphic techniques can be applied to a variety of procedures, thus storyboards both store and transfer knowledge. If HiPros are asked to provide coaching tips via a storyboard, they offer up their knowledge gained from experience. Storyboards are widely used in multimedia productions and in filmmaking. Many books on the subject describe how to develop and use storyboards, as well as offering a range of approaches to storyboard development.[8]

Mentoring Programs

A *mentor* is an experienced performer; a *mentee* is a less-experienced one. Rarely is a mentor a supervisor, since effective mentors should have no self-interest in the development of another person. Successful people have usually had one or more mentors in their careers, who have offered them advice on what to do, how to do it, and why it is worth doing. Such programs can, of course, facilitate knowledge transfer.

Mentoring programs may be planned or unplanned. In a planned mentoring program, the organization—usually the HR department—plays matchmaker, putting a less experienced person with someone in a different chain of command or department often two levels above. The HR department facilitates the introduction and may even provide training, or at least guidelines, to mentors and mentees about what to do in this relationship.

Mentoring programs have captured the attention of many decision makers because they seem to be well suited to efficient knowledge transfer. They also encourage individuals to take initiative for their own learning, rather than expecting the organization to spoon-feed them the training. Much has been written on mentoring and mentoring programs in recent years, as well as on designing these programs to accommodate knowledge transfer.[9]

Storytelling

Most wisdom in organizations is passed on through storytelling. In fact, it is sometimes said that corporate culture is best expressed through the stories told inside the organization. A story is a description of what happened in a situation. Most people have heard many stories about their organizations. If you hear "what really happened" in a promotion, demotion, termination, or transfer, you are hearing a story. Sometimes it takes the guise of gossip. Storytelling is less structured than critical incidents, but it can serve the same ends. It is a most effective way of transferring valuable knowledge from one person to another—such as from an in-house expert to a novice. Much has been written about storytelling in recent years as a technique to be used by leaders to effect change and by other people to dramatize what they teach.[10]

Information Exchanges

If you have ever attended a career fair, you have seen one form of information exchange. The same basic approach can be turned into organizational information exchanges. When this strategy is used, veteran performers sit at booths and dispense wisdom to less-experienced performers who visit them.

A simple way to set this up is to use round tables with signs indicating specific problems. You place a HiPro at each table who will talk about the problem. Then you ask novices to divide themselves up among the tables and go talk with the HiPros. Give a time frame, such as 15 or 30 minutes, and provide the novices with a list of questions to ask. At the end of that time, the novices rotate to other tables.

Best-Practice Studies or Meetings

Too often we assume that best practices occur outside our own organizations. But it is possible that our own organization has its own best practices, too. These can be shared internally via best-practice studies and in meetings. They can be the basis for knowledge transfer, sharing examples of how the organization performs at its best, who has done something well, and what lessons can be learned from what is being done right.

To begin, identify centers of excellence inside the organization. What departments, teams, or groups do specific things best? Select instances of strategic importance to the organization, such as departments that carry out work processes particularly well. Then, form a team to investigate exactly what they do, how they do it, and what they have learned from experience. Report the results in meetings, encouraging less experienced performers to attend and pose questions to the study team. It is, of course, best to have representatives available—in person or by teleconference—from the centers of excellence to answer questions and share experiences. Much has been written about conducting benchmarking and so designing a benchmarking study should not be that difficult.[11]

Training

Training can, of course, be a way to transfer knowledge. It is an obvious choice, and it is one that often occurs to many managers. But it is important to emphasize that knowledge transfer from HiPros to other workers will happen only when it is planned and is incorporated into the training design. Knowledge transfer can also be incorporated into planned on-the-job training, planned group training, or blended learning that includes online components.

After-Action Meetings

An *after-action meeting*—sometimes called an *after-action review*—is called after a project or a critical event, such as a major mistake in the production process, a disruption in service delivery, or the loss of a major client. In some industries—such as nuclear power—after-action meetings are required after critical events. But the same approach can be used in any industry as long as decision makers wish to do so. And the approach can be used to transfer knowledge, if that is the intention.

Most such meetings follow a standard format, which is simple and focused. The facilitators keep the group from placing blame and instead maintain the focus on exploring several key questions, such as:

♦ What was the goal to be achieved? (Clarify intentions and objectives)

♦ What happened? (Describe the situation as events unfolded, step by step)

♦ What lessons were learned? (Reflections on what happened, how similar situations should be handled in the future)

♦ What action will be taken? (How a similar event can be avoided)

Anyone who participated in an event—or even those who could benefit from knowledge in the future—may be involved in an after-action meeting. This reinforces what has been learned from experience, taking time to emphasize that learning.

DACUM Sessions

DACUM stands for Developing a Curriculum. Briefly stated, the approach involves bringing together a group of experienced performers to describe what they do on a daily basis. The result is a much more detailed job map than a typical job description, and from this occupational analysis, educators can develop a curriculum that effectively trains people to do a job. Trainers may even use it to present sequenced topics to learners in on-the-job training.

But DACUM can also be seen as knowledge transfer. You simply bring together a group of HiPros to describe how they do their work, ask them to list, step by step, what is necessary to carry out their projects, then have them provide coaching advice on each action step. The result is a map of the work with coaching tips provided by HiPros.

DACUM can be applied to members in one job category or to an entire team. It can also be combined with the critical-incident method, useful in detecting unusual make-or-break work situations. It should be apparent that, if HiPros are involved in describing their daily work, they will be helping transfer some of what they know to others.

Wikipedia

"*Wikipedia* is a multilingual, web-based, free-content encyclopedia project based on an openly-editable model. The name 'Wikipedia' is a portmanteau of the words wiki (a technology for creating collaborative websites, from the Hawaiian word wiki, meaning 'quick') and encyclopedia. Wikipedia's articles provide links to guide the user to related pages with additional information."[12] Similar Web-based encyclopedias can be built by the organization or developed on its intranet as a way to share knowledge. It then becomes a useful tool to transfer knowledge from HiPros to those possessing less knowledge or experience. These interactive resources promote collaborative development of content, and can become the medium for discussions about unique organizational problems or issues.

Blogs

As many people know, *blog* is short for *weblog*. A blog is an online log to which individuals make regular entries, much like a diary. People can update their blogs whenever they wish and can input words, videos, podcasts, or other media to record what they want others to read or see. If HiPros are encouraged to write blogs about what they have learned from their experience, especially about difficult or common work situations, then their blogs become a means for knowledge transfer. In December 2007, more than 112 million blogs were identified by the blog search engine Technorati. While blogs can be used in many ways, an organization's management can capitalize on their usefulness by asking workers to set them up for the expressed purpose of knowledge transfer.

Instant Messaging Programs

Instant messaging has rapidly become a critical part of our personal communications today, whether it is by text, video, or voice. Many such programs are available—such as Skype and Yahoo Messenger. If HiPros can be convinced to use instant messaging to convey what they have learned to others with less experience, then instant messaging programs can be effective in knowledge transfer. Instant messaging is already being used for real-time career counseling and executive coaching, and so it could easily be applied to knowledge transfer.

Social Networking and Chat Rooms

Social networking occurs when people get together and talk to each other. In the context of the twenty-first century, social networking is more often associated with online technology to connect people via social-network-ing Web sites. The best known sites are Facebook, MyFace, and MySpace. But many others also exist.

Chat rooms, an older technology, are still effective for connecting people. Some professional associations sponsor them for their members. They can be forums for transferring knowledge by encouraging those with experience to share with those who lack it. Organizational leaders can also establish them and use them for this purpose.

Mind Maps

A *mind map* is a picture meant to illustrate the relationships between and among ideas or concepts. It is not difficult to learn how to do mind-mapping.[13] If HiPros are asked to develop mind maps around important experiences, or are asked to chart what they have learned from their experiences, they are effectively mind-mapping and the results can be used by those with less learning.

World Café Programs

The "world café" is an approach to getting groups to interact and share information. Typically, people are brought together and gathered around tables. Large sheets of blank newsprint are placed on the tables. A facilitator poses questions and the group at the table discusses the possible answers, and then the participants write down their ideas on the newsprint. One person remains at each table from the original group and the others move on to other tables. This process is repeated several times, with a facilitator keeping time and reminding group members of what they should do. At the end, the newsprint from each table is posted on the wall. The facilitator then poses questions to participants to clarify what ideas have been surfaced by the groups.

This approach can, of course, easily be adapted to a knowledge-transfer session intended to pull technical or professional knowledge from HiPros and relay it to less experienced people. Care must be taken with the approach, however. Similar types of people, when brought together, will not necessarily achieve breakthrough innovative ideas. But if the approach is used simply, primarily for information sharing and knowledge transfer, it can be quite effective.[14]

Group Decision Support Systems (GDSS)

Group decision support systems (GDSS) are a technological innovation that facilitates information sharing among groups. First-generation approaches to GDSS assembled individuals in a room equipped with computers, a video projector, and special software. The facilitator posed questions, the participants typed their answers, and the facilitator helped the group to categorize its ideas and multi-vote on them. More recent generations of GDSS use Web-based technology to enable virtual teams to participate in these sessions and incorporate text messaging technology, which permits very large groups to share their thoughts on video projectors, resulting in large-scale decision making. An important value of GDSS is that ideas are regarded apart from the rank and status of the individuals involved.

Today, we can use GDSS technology to transfer knowledge from HiPros to less experienced people. You simply bring the HiPros together—or ask them to meet virtually—and pose questions about what they have learned from their experience. You facilitate the discussion and help them identify and prioritize the information that should be transferred, as well as develop ways to do that.[15]

Expert Systems

Less practical than some other approaches to knowledge transfer, largely because it is more time-consuming and expensive to develop, an expert system is organized around problems and how to troubleshoot them to find solutions. It is usually automated, but it does not have to be. A simple example of an expert system is the "context-sensitive help" on most word processing programs. Similarly, if you call in to the help desk of a major computer company, the person on the other end is probably equipped with an expert system to guide him or her in providing you with answers to your problem.

In an expert system, common or difficult problems are logged in. The expert knowledge is also logged in to a computer system, cross-referenced to the problems. Troubleshooting advice and possible solutions are matched to the problems. While requiring more technological sophistication to establish the program, this approach places expert information at the fingertips of even the least experienced performer, giving him or her ability to perform like a pro. Building an expert system is an effective, but time-consuming and expensive, way to facilitate knowledge transfer.[16]

Performance Support Systems

Perhaps the most sophisticated (and thus most expensive and time-consuming to develop) of all methods for storing and transferring knowledge is the *electronic performance support system* (EPSS). An EPSS combines artificial intelligence, an expert system, real-time e-learning methods, and a computer-based referencing system. As users encounter problems, they find at their fingertips all the help they need electronically to answer their questions—such as organizational policies and procedures through the referencing system, knowledge from the expert system, online training and real-time coaching, and artificial intelligence to help guide the users to the information. Obviously, such a system would be a fabulous way to transfer knowledge and ensure that it is used in real time. HiPros can be encouraged to review the operations of the performance support system to enhance it.[17]

Other Strategies

There are, of course, other ways to store and/or transfer knowledge than to use the strategies listed above. One way for an organization's decision makers to capture the lessons of experience is to do better than they have historically done in tapping their retiree base.[18] Individuals with valuable knowledge can be placed on retainers, available to provide one-on-one phone guidance—or even online or video-conferenced advice. Managing the retiree base of the organization may prove to be an important trend of the future. It may also be possible to involve former technical and professional workers in brainstorming ways to transfer their knowledge to current workers.

Chapter Summary

This chapter listed two dozen ways that knowledge transfer can be facilitated. While not all approaches can or should be used in every situation, it should be apparent that there is no lack of means for doing it. The real questions are these: (1) How willing is management to commit the time, money, and staff to a knowledge transfer effort? (2) Which methods might be most appropriate—and practical—to a specific application? and (3) How supportive are HiPros of providing information they have gained from experience?

Use the assessment tool in Exhibit 8-2 to consider the range of methods that may be applicable to one department or group, and pinpoint the best approaches to transferring knowledge.

EXHIBIT 8-2.

TOOL FOR ASSESSING WAYS TO TRANSFER KNOWLEDGE.

Directions: For each approach listed in the left-hand column, rate how practical and useful it would be for the group targeted for knowledge transfer. Use this scale: *0 = Not appropriate; 1 = Not at all practical/useful; 2 = Somewhat practical/useful; 3 = Practical/useful; 4 = Very practical and useful.* Compare respondents' scores to reveal themes and use as the basis for establishing a program.

Approach to Knowledge Transfer	How Practical and Useful for the Targeted Group?					*Notes*
	0	*1*	*2*	*3*	*4*	
1. Job shadowing	0	1	2	3	4	
2. Job switching	0	1	2	3	4	
3. Job rotation	0	1	2	3	4	
4. Communities of practice	0	1	2	3	4	
5. Process documentation	0	1	2	3	4	
6. Critical incident interviews/ questionnaires	0	1	2	3	4	
7. Job aids	0	1	2	3	4	
8. Storyboards	0	1	2	3	4	
9. Mentoring programs	0	1	2	3	4	
10. Storytelling	0	1	2	3	4	
11. Information exchanges	0	1	2	3	4	
12. Best-practice studies or meetings	0	1	2	3	4	
13. Training	0	1	2	3	4	
14. After-action meetings	0	1	2	3	4	
15. DACUM sessions	0	1	2	3	4	

continues)

EXHIBIT 8-2. (continued)

Approach to Knowledge Transfer	How Practical and Useful for the Targeted Group?					Notes
	0	1	2	3	4	
16. Wikipedias	0	1	2	3	4	
17. Blogs	0	1	2	3	4	
18. Instant messaging programs	0	1	2	3	4	
19. Social networking and chat rooms	0	1	2	3	4	
20. Mind maps	0	1	2	3	4	
21. World café programs	0	1	2	3	4	
22. Group decision support systems (GDSS)	0	1	2	3	4	
23. Expert systems	0	1	2	3	4	
24. Performance support systems	0	1	2	3	4	
25. Tapping retirees of the organization	0	1	2	3	4	

9.

Tackling Future Challenges

What challenges in the future will those interested in technical and professional talent management confront? This chapter offers twenty-five predictions regarding the future of technical and professional talent management. While not all of them may apply to your organization, probably at least some of them will. You'll want to be prepared for those that can impact your organization.

The Future of TTM—Some Predictions

Review these predictions to determine their importance to your organization, an exercise included here as Exhibit 9-1, and then read about the resolutions to any predictions that could become possible problems.

HiPros Will Become Increasingly Important for the Organization's Competitiveness

If it is true that talent is becoming the only real basis for competitive advantage, then organizational leaders will increasingly devote attention

(text continues on page 150)

EXHIBIT 9-1.

WORKSHEET FOR ASSESSING TRENDS IN TTM.

Directions: For each trend listed in the left-hand column, indicate how important it is to your organization. Use this scale in rating importance: *0 = Not applicable to this organization; 1 = Not at all important to this organization; 2 = Somewhat important to this organization; 3 = Important to this organization; and 4 = Very important to this organization.* There are no right or wrong answers per se. However, some trends may have more impact on your organization—or on some departments—than others. Add other trends that may affect your organization's best technical and professional workers. Share your perceptions with others in the organization.

	Importance to Your Organization				
Trends	*Not Applicable*	*Not At All Important*	*Somewhat Important*	*Important*	*Very Important*
1. HiPros will become increasingly important for the organization's competitiveness.	0	1	2	3	4
2. Effective HiPros will keep pace with technological innovations.	0	1	2	3	4
3. Organizations will focus on quantity and quality of technical/ professional support.	0	1	2	3	4
4. Workforce planning will balance technical expertise with leadership ability.	0	1	2	3	4
5. Technical and professional competence will require customization.	0	1	2	3	4
6. Rapidly finding specialized talent will grow increasingly important.	0	1	2	3	4
7. Dual career ladders will become more common.	0	1	2	3	4
8. Creative approaches to HR will be used more often.	0	1	2	3	4
9. Workers will demand more challenging work.	0	1	2	3	4
10. The socialization of prospective and new recruits will require more attention.	0	1	2	3	4

Trends	Importance to Your Organization				
	Not Applicable	Not At All Important	Somewhat Important	Important	Very Important
11. Retirees will become a brain trust to preserve unique knowledge.	0	1	2	3	4
12. Talent management will accommodate special needs and status.	0	1	2	3	4
13. Management of technical/ professional workers will require distinct competencies.	0	1	2	3	4
14. Innovators and those who inspire others will be in greatest demand.	0	1	2	3	4
15. Effective interpersonal skills will be critical.	0	1	2	3	4
16. HiPros will serve as mentors.	0	1	2	3	4
17. Technical/professional workers will feel more loyalty to their fields than to employers.	0	1	2	3	4
18. Development efforts for technical/ professional workers will begin early and will continue.	0	1	2	3	4
19. Performance management will focus on long-term contributions.	0	1	2	3	4
20. Reward systems will be based on results, behaviors, and ethics.	0	1	2	3	4
21. Selection systems will emphasize teamwork and complex work structures.	0	1	2	3	4
22. Selection systems will favor unique gifts or talents.	0	1	2	3	4
23. Knowledge transfer will be essential for good management.	0	1	2	3	4
24. Knowledge transfer will expand to all workers.	0	1	2	3	4
25. Organizations will be at high risk when they lose valuable employees.	0	1	2	3	4
26. Other trends:					

not just to those who are promotable but also to those who are in-house experts on business issues unique to the organization. Organizational leaders will devote more time and attention to defining business problems, identifying those who possess special knowledge or competence for solving those problems, capturing their knowledge, and transferring that knowledge to others. This action and outlook will be apparent because retirements are occurring at a rapid rate.

Every organization has one or more core competencies—that is, what it does better than competitors or others in the same industry. Without that core competency, the organization has no competitive advantage. Indeed, the core competency is the unique strategic strength of the organization. In-house experts of many kinds may exist, but those most important are those who possess knowledge that is mission critical to preserving and leveraging competitive advantage.

Perhaps a simple example will illustrate. A company that manufactures cell phones requires a workforce that is aware of the business. That is understood to be a given. But some people possess unique knowledge about how the organization solved the problems that led to the current generation of cell phones. That knowledge may be critical to moving to a future generation of cell phones. Hence, individuals who possess special knowledge that is critical to business continuity are the most important in-house experts. They are the ones who should be identified and every effort made to capture and transfer what they know to others.

The importance of high professionals who possess knowledge unique to the business and to the organization's core competency will grow increasingly important in the future. Generally speaking, they cannot be hired from outside; they must be developed from within. And, of course, gaining experience takes time. Hence, planning for their loss and for transferring what they know is becoming "mission critical" for many organizations if they are to preserve their competitive advantage.

What should you and your organization do about this prediction? Identify what the organization's core competency is, and then pinpoint those who possess the most valuable knowledge related to sustaining or enhancing that core competency. Do that in talent review meetings.

Effective HiPros Will Keep Pace with Technological Innovations

Talent is a wasting asset, just like equipment. Knowledge—even specialized knowledge—does not remain current forever. It must be refreshed through a range of methods, including cross-pollination of in-house experts, training, continuing education, and uninterrupted exposure to new ideas and shifting business conditions. In tomorrow's world, the best talent will remain current with new developments, and those who do not will no longer be useful to the organization. Just as one person may not forever be considered promotable because business requirements change, so too technical and professionals will not forever be considered in-house experts unless their knowledge and experience remain useful.

Organizations Will Focus on Quantity and Quality of Technical/Professional Support

Workforce planning involves examining the number and type (quantity and quality) of people required to produce desired results. As experience with many downsizings has shown, organizational leaders are not always fully aware of *whom* they are losing when they "cut heads" to save money. The old saying that "everybody is replaceable" has its limitations. For instance, replacing some people can be particularly painful because they may be more productive or more creative than their peers.

In the future, organizational leaders will devote more time and attention to planning for the quantity and quality of people they need to achieve strategic objectives. That will require more robust approaches to workforce planning than have been typical in the past. And much attention will be paid to individuals whose talents are regarded as technical or professional. For instance, in banks, commercial mortgage lending is a

What should you and your organization do about this prediction? Start now to develop competency inventories—inventories that include retirees as well as active workers, so that the organization has as many possible experts available to deal with a crisis.

Dual Career Ladders Will Become More Common

Organizations compete for talent. And periodically there are global shortages of talent in some specialized groups, such as engineers, IT professionals, or medical professionals. Organizations wanting to compete for that talent—and/or want to retain it—must do more than offer quick pay raises based on time in position. Dual career ladders will be the way organizations will attract and retain talent as well as recognize professional achievement. Recognition via horizontal promotion will increase as organizations delayer management positions in an effort to cut costs and reduce decision-making time.

What should you and your organization do about this prediction? Experiment with dual career ladders. Do not expect that any one approach will be perfect—especially when it is first unveiled. But start now and try various paths to dual career ladders.

Creative Approaches to HR Will Be Used More Often

Organizations that rely on traditional approaches to recruiting, developing, and retaining their technical and professional workers will get only mediocre results. After all, doing what everyone else does will not give an organization a unique employment brand or attract people in technical or professional fields. The organizations that will succeed in attracting, developing, and retaining talent will be those that adopt creative approaches that will appeal to new graduates—and to experienced talent.

What should you and your organization do about this prediction? Form a task force of recent hires. Ask them how the organization can establish an enviable reputation as an employer. Come up with a proposal to do that, and then implement it.

Workers Will Demand More Challenging Work

Already, many organizations report that departing technical and professional workers less often cite salary and more often lack of sufficient challenge as their chief reason for leaving. Managing the challenges given to new hires—as well as to people at every stage of their careers—is critical to talent retention, yet it is an issue not always addressed in performance reviews or in individual development plans. In the future, organizational leaders will devote time and attention to managing the expectations of workers for professional challenge.

What should you and your organization do about this prediction? Pose questions about professional challenge during recruitment and selection; address the matter of professional challenge during onboarding; consider these challenges during annual individual-development planning processes; make sure the subject is covered during performance reviews; include questions about challenges on employee climate surveys; and ask about it during exit interviews.

The Socialization of Prospective and New Recruits Will Require More Attention

Many business observers agree that onboarding—sometimes called socialization—is a process, not a program. Already, many organizations devote much time and attention to onboarding. Savvy recruiters also realize that socialization begins during recruitment and selection, and it continues for as long as the worker is employed. Socialization can also continue after employment, since some organizations such as IBM have alumni groups. In fact, some organizations attempt to recapture their lost talent, "stealing back" people lost to other employers. Increasingly, organizational leaders will spend even more time managing the experiences of their technical and professional workers because that is critical to developing and retaining that talent.

What should you and your organization do about this prediction? Follow the advice for the previous prediction: pose questions about pro-

fessional challenge during the recruitment and selection; address professional challenge during onboarding; discuss challenge during annual
individual-development planning processes; include it during performance reviews; ask questions about it on employee-climate surveys; and
delve into it during exit interviews.

Retirees Will Become a Brain Trust to Preserve Unique Knowledge

In the future, retirement will be different from how it is today. Many
workers cannot afford to retire completely; escalating healthcare costs
alone make that unrealistic. And employers often discover that, once
someone retires, they overestimated how easily it would be to replace that
person. A convergence of trends makes it likely that employers will stay
in touch with their retirees and attempt to draw on their knowledge for
short-term, virtual, and long-term assignments. Retirees will be included
in organizational talent inventories so that their special knowledge can be
tapped as needed, especially in a crisis.

What should you and your organization do about this situation?
Launch efforts to stay in touch with retirees right now, and periodically
into the future. Form company alumni groups to encourage retirees to
stay connected. Find out what the retirees can and want to do, then take
steps to involve them as needed.

Talent Management Will Accommodate Special Needs and Status

Many talent-management programs have prepared HiPos for promotion.
But it is likely that these programs will change to capturing, preserving,
and distilling special knowledge. The HiPros will serve as mentors to
HiPos and also as resources for HiPros-in-preparation. Already some organizations run special programs for uniquely talented professionals focused on increasing technical innovation and transferring knowledge, as
well as preparing individuals for more challenging technical projects.
They are designed somewhat differently from in-house HiPo programs

intended to prepare people for future leadership responsibilities. Preferably, there should be some overlap between management and technical talent management programs. Future leaders can learn from in-house experts; future HiPros can learn leadership and management skills.

What should you and your organization do about this prediction? Establish HiPro programs to match the HiPo programs. Draw attention to the special value that professional and technical know-how plays in corporate success, as well as the promotability of technical talent.

Management of Technical/Professional Workers Will Require Distinct Competencies

When it comes to managing workers, does one size fit all? I do not think so. Managing talented technical and professional workers is different from managing other workers. For one thing, managers of technical and professional workers need sufficient knowledge to enjoy credibility with those they oversee. But does that mean these managers must excel at that work? No, they should have the ability to encourage people who may be quite proud of their technical skills and may act like prima donnas. Successful managers of technical people know how to ask tough questions, how to use humor, and how to boost people when they feel discouraged. No doubt additional research should be done on the special competencies required of those who manage technical and professional workers, as this will be only more prevalent in coming decades.

What should you and your organization do about this prediction? Conduct a competency study of especially good managers of technical and professional workers. Use that research to isolate what makes them so good, and then use that information in recruiting, selecting, and developing managers of technical and professional workers.

Innovators and Those Who Inspire Others Will Be in Greatest Demand

The ability to innovate—or to encourage innovation in others—is not traditionally taught in school. Yet, most observers of the contemporary business scene agree that the ability to innovate, and then come up with commercial applications for new ideas, is and will be the most important competitive factor in the future. Technical and professional workers who can be innovative, and inspire others to innovate, will be in greatest demand. But finding these workers is not always easy. Those who can innovate are usually on the periphery of the business world and are less accepting of its structure. Consider Bill Gates, Steven Jobs, and Michael Dell, all of whom dropped out of college. Albert Einstein failed a college entrance exam. Mozart never attended school. Successful innovators do not follow the conventional wisdom and often do not have the necessary qualifications.

To identify future talent, investigate how the talented people in the organization came to be that way. Ask others who the most innovative people are, and then discover what characteristics they share. Use those characteristics—those competencies—as a basis for recruiting, developing, and retaining talent, identifying likewise whose special expertise may be worth transferring to others. Remember that the best judge of innovation is not the immediate supervisor but, rather, technical and professional peers.

What should you and your organization do about this prediction? Identify and then study the people in your organization who are regarded as the most innovative. Interview them to look for patterns, and then use that information on a test basis to see if it helps to recruit, select, and develop innovative people in the future.

Effective Interpersonal Skills Will Be Critical

Over the years, many leaders have noticed that technical and professional workers sometimes lack interpersonal skills. This should really come as no surprise; individuals who are good at working with and analyzing data are drawn to occupations in engineering, research science, and IT work. But to be promotable, these workers must be able to work with and through others.

This problem has been studied. For instance, "research with professional engineers in New Zealand, including a training needs analysis, has indicated a strong need and high potential benefits from management training, particularly in personal and interpersonal management skills."[1] Another study conducted in Taiwan found that "engineers' interpersonal skills significantly moderate the influences of customer orientation of collaborations on their innovation performances, but do not significantly moderate the influences from the technology orientation of collaborations."[2]

In the future, organizations will carefully examine the interpersonal skills of technical and professional workers as a point in recruitment, development, and retention. They will also devise methods—such as coaching—to help individuals improve their ability to interact with others. Interpersonal skills will continue to grow as a critical competency because so much technical work is done on teams or by virtual teams.

What should you and your organization do about this prediction? Conduct role plays with technical and professional job applicants to see how often and how well they interact with others. Even just simply counting how often they interact with others at a reception might be an indication of interpersonal skills.

HiPros Will Serve as Mentors

Not everyone has what it takes to be an effective mentor. A mentor is a teacher who has a self-interest in another person's development. Some organizations have developed formal (planned) mentoring programs, but much of the research suggests that successful people seek out one or more others to mentor them and they are willing to take the initiative to do so. In the future, organizational leaders will encourage HiPros to mentor others. Of course, to do so they will have to overcome several obstacles, the first of which is a HiPro's unwillingness to serve as a mentor. Not everyone can be a mentor; it starts with a willingness to help others. Those who have no interest in, or sympathy for, others will find the task an onerous one.

Organizations must also make mentoring worthwhile for those who engage in it. If HiPros have to choose between doing their work and teaching others, common sense tells you which they will choose. Additionally, as organizations downsize, HiPros worry that if they give away their knowledge, they will also reduce their chances of staying. Whether that is realistic or not does not matter; what does matter are perceptions. So, organizational leaders must be willing to recognize—and reward—mentoring according to one or many ways that will make it of value to those who undertake it.

What should you and your organization do about this prediction? Establish and maintain a mentoring program in your organization. Train individuals how to be good mentors; and train workers how to make best use of mentors.

Technical/Professional Workers Will Feel More Loyalty to Their Field Than to Employers

Many organizations lament the loss of employee loyalty. Younger workers in particular are singled out, accused of having interest only in their immediate, short-term prospects. They are too mercenary, some say. But those who complain about deficient worker loyalty ignore the effects of downsizing that has characterized business for many years. These younger workers have often seen their parents become victims of downsizing, after decades of loyal service. So it is understandable that workers will be loyal to themselves and to their professions rather than to their employers. That trend will continue as long as downsizing is used by employers to cut costs. Similarly, continuing education programs established by professional associations will grow in influence, for the simple reason that workers will trust their professional association more than they do their employers *du jour*.

What does this mean? Workers will need to be challenged in order to stay with the company, and feedback and rewards must be more visible and given more rapidly.

Development of Technical/Professional Workers Will Begin Early and Continue

Development of technical and professional skills will vary with the individual. An organization needs to take personal strengths into consideration and not necessarily put every technical and professional worker on the same path.

What should you and your organization do about this prediction? Study patterns for success among the HiPros. In some instances, underlying gender differences may matter and should be considered in development programs for men and women in the organization and determine if there are particular reasons why women may not be advancing as rapidly as men. Address any gender opportunity differences in your developmental programs.

Performance Management Will Focus on Long-Term Contributions

Many years ago, HR guru Elliott Jacques invented the term *time span of discretion*.[3] First applied to salary studies, this is the time between starting a work task or duty and completing it. According to Jacques, an hourly worker might have a time span of discretion of an hour; a middle manager of one year; and a CEO as much as twenty years. (Today the time span for CEOs is much less!) In essence, it can function as a measure of responsibility in a job.

For technical and professional workers, the time spans of discretion may vary, depending on the project. Major technological innovations can take many years to pay off; for example, it can take fifteen years to bring a new drug to market.[4] An overemphasis on short-term gains at an organization may actually impede long-term results. The organization's performance management must acknowledge the long lead time for seeing results from its technical and professional staff—a trend that will only increase in strength in the coming years.

What should you and your organization do about this prediction?

Encourage management questions about employee development that ex-
tend beyond annual time periods. Long-term as well as short-term developmental paths will help technical and professional employees contribute
to the organization's long-term success.

Reward Systems Will Be Based on Results, Behaviors, and Ethics

Tomorrow's reward systems for technical and professional workers will
emphasize results achieved, behaviors demonstrated, and particularly ad-
herence to ethical standards. Ethics has emerged as a matter of growing
importance in business. It is not enough to get good results.[5] Managers—
and their technical and professional workers—must adhere to high moral
standards in getting those results. Reward systems (including promotion
decisions) will increasingly include consideration of ethical behavior, in
addition to demonstrated results.

While the most high-profile ethical abuses that have surfaced in the
press concern CEOs, technical and professional workers have not been
immune from ethical lapses. The *Challenger* disaster resulted from an
ethical dilemma faced by engineers; the Kansas City Hyatt Regency hotel
walkways collapse was possibly caused by taking shortcuts on engineering
specifications; and Arthur Andersen's ethical lapse in applying generally
accepted accounting principles resulted in the organization's demise.
Many examples exist of compromises made to meet tight deadlines, of
falsifying results, and similar violations of ethics.

Talent management programs will need to increase efforts to assess
individual behavior and look for ethics violations. That will require understanding of ethical dilemmas faced by the workers. To begin, survey
workers about critical incidents in which their ethics were called into
question. Then analyze the responses to discover common themes and
address those through management action, policy, and training. There
should also be a publicized code of conduct, emphasized in recruitment
and development, and ethical behavior measured against those standards
for determining appraisal and retention.

Selection Systems Will Emphasize Teamwork and Complex Work Structures

Traditional selection systems focus on how well workers will be able to carry out the responsibilities cited in the job description and how well applicants meet minimum education, experience, and other entry requirements. Job descriptions usually emphasize individual responsibilities but often do describe contributions via teamwork. And yet today, and into the future, much work is done by teams, whether virtual or in-house, and in complex structures such as matrix organizations.

Interpersonal skills are critical to success in both team settings and matrix structures. Selection systems need also to address how well job applicants can do their jobs on a team or in a complex structure. Yet interpersonal skills and communication is an area of traditional weakness for technical and professional workers.

What should you and your organization do about this prediction? Ask the job applicants how they have dealt with complicated interpersonal situations in the past. For example, "Tell me about a time when you were on a work project with a difficult interpersonal situation. What did you do? What happened as a result?" Questions such as these may help identify people who can thrive in a complicated organizational environment.

Selection Systems Will Favor Unique Gifts or Talents

A concept first suggested by C. K. Prahalad and Gary Hamel, a *core competency* is something that is central to a business—that it does better than other businesses, that is not easy for them to duplicate, and that can be leveraged to strategic advantage.[6] Core competency is perhaps most easily understood as the essence of what makes an organization successful.

Individuals also have core competencies. An idea consistent with the *strengths-based* approach to management, the term suggests that every individual has a unique talent that sets him or her apart from others.[7] The difficulty comes when you need to identify that talent and apply it to the organization's advantage. Not all strengths are useful to an organization or good for a particular job.

Consider these questions:

♦ What does that individual do better than other people?

♦ What is the individual passionate about?

♦ How does the individual recognize his or her own strengths?

♦ How can a manager recognize the strengths in his or her people?

In the future, organizational leaders will look at workers as teams of individuals rather than as isolated job incumbents. Thus, unique strengths that individuals bring to a team should be considered during the selection process.[8] Leveraging the strengths of individuals as members of teams will be essential for technical and professional work.

What should you and your organization do about this? Include interviews with team members during the selection interviews. Team members should be trained to look for team skills and then measure the job applicants against those requirements.

Knowledge Transfer Will Be Essential for Good Management

Fewer than 40 percent of U.S. organizations presently make any effort to transfer knowledge. The old idea that "everyone can be replaced" has yet to die. Of course, everyone *can* be replaced, but a person's successor may possess only a modicum of the knowledge his or her predecessors had. And it is equally likely that, if no effort is made to isolate that knowledge, distill it, and find practical ways to transfer it, the organization will suffer.

The danger is real. The organization whose workforce has a long average tenure is most at risk. If a large group of people retire in a short time span, the organization might actually "forget" how to do its most basic tasks. Managers of technical and professional workers are often sensitive to this problem, but their supervisors may not feel similarly or be able to see the consequences that can result from losing institutional memory.

What should you and your organization do about this prediction? Give this book to key decision makers or brief them on its contents. Write a short white paper on the subject and distribute it to the decision makers. In short, raise awareness of the dangers involved in losing invaluable knowledge. Stress the importance of knowledge transfer.

Knowledge Transfer Will Expand to All Workers

In a knowledge-based economy, knowledge is what counts most. That would appear to be a truism, but the reality is different: knowledge of value to the organization is not confined to technical and professional workers. Many people have valuable knowledge. In fact, it is possible that everyone in the organization does. It is all a matter of identifying what is important knowledge.

Many organizations need to devote more time and attention to *knowledge management*, defined as the process of managing information and knowledge essential to business success and operations. Knowledge management is bigger than technical succession planning, which is the process of identifying, distilling, and transferring knowledge that is at risk of loss as people retire, become disabled, or resign. Knowledge management guarantees that valuable knowledge is not lost or discarded.

What should you and your organization do about this prediction? Mount efforts to pinpoint the unique strengths—the value added—of each employee. What can each individual do better than the others, and how does that special ability positively affect the organization? Include that information in competency inventories.

Organizations Will Be at High Risk When They Lose Valuable Employees

As organizational leaders become sensitized to the catastrophic loss that can result from the sudden death, resignation, disability, or retirement of

HiPros, they will be more willing to take action. Collecting evidence is critical to that end. To avoid sounding like Chicken Little, you can pose a simple question: "What would happen if we lost _____?" That question alone may be sufficient to dramatize the problem for some senior managers. Specific people are known to be in-house experts, and the risk of their loss can be a frightening prospect for those aware of what they know and have done.

Other people—perhaps those not so closely in touch with operations—will require more evidence in the form of (for instance) charts that show estimated retirement eligibility dates for core business departments. Another way is to follow up after a valuable person leaves the organization, asking the person's former manager what problems have resulted from the loss. Collect information like this over time and present it to key decision makers.

What to Do Next

Now that you have read the predictions, begin some action planning to deal with them. Use the worksheet in Exhibit 9-2 to consider what your organization can do to address these issues.

Chapter Summary

This chapter offered twenty-five likely predictions about the future of technical and professional talent management. Each prediction was accompanied by potential solutions and adaptation methods, with the hope that your proposals stemming from them will provide the outline for decision makers to enter the future well prepared.

EXHIBIT 9-2.

WORKSHEET FOR ADDRESSING TRENDS IN TTM.

Directions: For each trend listed in the left-hand column, list specific actions your organization should take to address the trend. Remember that some trends may have more impact on your organization—or on some departments—than on others. Add other trends at the end of this worksheet. Be prepared to share your action plans with others in the organization.

Trends	*Action Plans*
1. HiPros will become increasingly important for the organization's competitiveness.	
2. Effective HiPros will keep pace with technological innovations.	
3. Organizations will focus on quantity and quality of technical/professional support.	
4. Workforce planning will balance technical expertise with leadership ability.	
5. Technical and professional competence will require customization.	
6. Rapidly finding specialized talent will grow increasingly important.	
7. Dual career ladders will become more common.	
8. Creative approaches to HR will be used more often.	
9. Workers will demand more challenging work.	
10. The socialization of prospective and new recruits will require more attention.	
11. Retirees will become a brain trust to preserve unique knowledge.	
12. Talent management will accommodate special needs and status.	

Trends	Action Plans
13. Management of technical/professional workers will require distinct competencies.	
14. Innovators and those who inspire others will be in greatest demand.	
15. Effective interpersonal skills will be critical.	
16. HiPros will serve as mentors.	
17. Technical/ professional workers will feel more loyalty to their fields than to employers.	
18. Development efforts for technical/ professional workers will begin early and will continue.	
19. Performance management will focus on long-term contributions.	
20. Reward systems will be based on results, behaviors, and ethics.	
21. Selection systems will emphasize teamwork and complex work structures.	
22. Selection systems will favor unique gifts or talents.	
23. Knowledge transfer will be essential for good management.	
24. Knowledge transfer will expand to all workers.	
25. Organizations will be at high risk when they lose valuable employees.	
Other trends:	

Appendix I

Cases in Technical and Professional Talent Management

Farsighted leaders have been thinking for some years about knowledge transfer and other special issues associated with technical talent management. Presented here are a range of cases, some of them especially good and some demonstrating how organizational leaders have struggled with the problem.

CASE STUDY 1

Stopping Brain Drain

By Larry Dignan

SOURCE: From "Stopping Brain Drain," *Baseline* 1, no. 47 (2005): 708–33. Used by permission.

Twelve hundred of the 3,700 employees who work for Bruce Power, a utility company in Tiverton, Ontario, are eligible to retire in the next three years. CEO Duncan Hawthorne sees that as a threat—and an opportunity.

The threat: Retirees leave with more than two decades of knowledge about Bruce Power's reactors, how those units are maintained, and all the little items—such as the quirks of an aging steam generator and ways to weld metals that have been altered by extreme heat—that can't be found in textbooks. The opportunity: Infuse Canada's first private nuclear power generator with new blood, thinking, and technical skills.

Simply put, the generator of 20 percent of Ontario's power could come apart almost literally at its seams. Hawthorne can, of course, afford to lose the retirees' salaries. What he can't afford to lose is what's in their heads. "These workers were here in the mid-1970s when the site was commissioned and the boilers were installed," Hawthorne says. "They have the full history. We can replace the certifications, but not the tricks of the trade and the skills of a craftsman. We don't want to lose that corporate knowledge."

His answer? Making "sure we've sucked dry the experience of workers before they leave." His tool? A knowledge database created using Kana Software's IQ application. When finished, the company will have access to information on everything from how to weld steam-pipe fittings and their supports, to how to perform an exit interview properly, to work-arounds for repairing an office printer.

A knowledge management project might seem like a no-brainer, but it's hard to quantify, according to Jim Murphy, an analyst at AMR Research. First, a system has to be developed so it can apply to multiple parts of the business, such as human resources and plant maintenance. Then you need employees to use the system and deliver their knowledge by inputting tips into a Web form. Even if that goes well, measuring returns on sharing experience and saving time isn't easy.

Nevertheless, Murphy says knowledge management software is being used in businesses that have a large number of pending retirees and where operating efficiencies or a competitive advantage such as a novel R&D technique can be promised. A pharmaceutical company, for instance, can't just let the scientist who has developed a patented drug defect to a rival.

The rub: "It's an inexact way of approaching the problem, but it's better than nothing," Murphy says.

Hawthorne says most of Bruce Power's returns are anecdotal—a crew, say, that used information from the knowledge base to save an hour on a reactor repair. But there aren't any hard numbers linking knowledge management to the end result. "We track work crew tasks, compare crews, and look at errors and time to completion, but it's hard to say how much can be attributed directly to knowledge management," he says.

However, Hawthorne sees knowledge management as a necessity. And supervisors can create and maintain metrics that will give some idea of the benefits produced.

Murphy says most companies using knowledge management software try to calculate returns based on phone calls saved, time saved—say, 15 minutes a day—or lower training costs. But that assumes you could put a value on saved time, and employees used the time for work. "If I had an extra four minutes a day, what would I really do with it?" Murphy asks.

Hawthorne went ahead with the knowledge-management project because it serves as an insurance policy. "We can never be in a position of not knowing how to do something," he says. "This allows older workers to pass along skills and help train future workers."

Christophe Michel, manager of technology solutions at Bruce Power, says the company began its knowledge management rollout slowly in early 2002 by focusing on human resources. The problem: Bruce Power had too many phone calls about policies governing vacation time and benefits. The fix was developing a portal that could handle the most basic questions and free up managers for more complicated queries.

The project, completed in November 2002, served as a template for a dozen areas, ranging from welding to strategic issues such as company positions on the environment and technology support.

According to Michel, each knowledge base has the same look and feel, and includes Web forms to allow workers to input "knowledge deliverables" about a specific activity. For instance, a report on a turbine repair would include the job, time to complete it, and details on any hurdles, such as metal that unexpectedly fused, and how they were overcome. The data are shared across the company and, in some cases, the nuclear power industry, which shares information about plant operations since the Three Mile Island meltdown in 1979.

The challenge is convincing employees that sharing knowledge about something like maintaining the brackets that hold steam pipes in a generator is important. "The success of knowledge management might be 20 to 30 percent technology, and the rest is process and culture," Michel says. "The most significant hurdle is changing the attitudes toward daily work."

Hawthorne says the goal is to capture data on jobs that don't occur daily—say, restarting a steam generator after an outage. He says that knowledge is the most likely information to be lost as retirees walk off into the sunset.

If all goes well, Hawthorne says Bruce Power will retain its corporate culture and provide road maps to do both routine and once-in-a-decade tasks. Hawthorne likens knowledge management to the difference between getting directions from Mapquest and from a local truck driver. "You can print a map that gives you a route; that's easy," Hawthorne says. "But that route won't tell you where the construction is unless you get directions from someone who has traveled that route. We're trying to retain that knowledge."

Bruce Power collects employee experience with knowledge management software.

CASE STUDY 2

Building a Talent Pipeline

By B. Goretsky and D. Pettry

SOURCE: From "Building a Talent Pipeline," *T + D* 61, no. 6 (2007): 57–62. Used by permission.

Dusko Dragojlovic, an engineering director at Northrop Grumman, knew the focus he wanted to take for his team's planning retreat. Leading a

team of more than 1,000 engineers and technicians, he and his direct
reports needed to make recruitment, retention, and development of talent their top priorities in 2007. If the issues were not addressed, his sector
could lose its competitive edge. He passionately believed this and had the
data to back up his beliefs. The challenge was to get the team to see what
he saw.

Dragojlovic succeeded in convincing his managers that high turnover
posed a threat to the company. Each of his subordinates took responsibility for creating a project team that included engineers and technicians of
varying tenure and expertise to address a key talent issue for 2007. Dragojlovic now receives monthly progress reports in his management meetings.

Dragojlovic is not the only line manager at Northrop Grumman to
understand and act upon the issue. Results from a recent company survey
revealed that 100 percent of the director-level respondents "view the
human capital skills issue as a critical management issue for the company."

Limited Talent Supply

When Jack Northrop started his airplane manufacturing business in 1939,
he had no idea that it would become a global defense and technology
company with more than 122,000 employees worldwide.

After a decade of mergers and acquisitions concluded in 2003, Northrop Grumman acquired twenty-two different companies and divided
them into eight business sectors. Integrating the various cultures into one
enterprise became a top strategic priority for the company.

As the company continued to shape its strategy, it confronted some
of the same challenges its competitors did in finding, developing, and
retaining talent. The company offers knowledge-intensive work that attracts scientists, engineers, computer scientists, and skilled production
employees seeking opportunities to contribute to national security efforts.

However, it was apparent that future employees would be in short supply when many current employees retire in the near future.

Northrop Grumman's problem was complicated by a talent pool that is smaller than in many other industries because most of the company's work requires national security clearances, which require engineers and scientists to be U.S. citizens.

These challenges forced company leaders to pose the following questions:

♦ How do we close the human capital gap?

♦ How do we close it better and faster than the competition?

♦ How do we involve line management in the solution, so that it is not just a human resources issue?

♦ How do we do this without laying yet another initiative on overworked leaders?

Enabling Event

Northrop Grumman created an executive development program called LEADING One Northrop Grumman, to address these issues. During 2004 and 2005, all vice presidents attended this weeklong executive development program, which is composed of a leadership competency model of skills needed to support the new culture of collaboration. The program included team-based learning assignments that focused on urgent competitive business problems. These assignments enabled participants to collaborate on strategic needs. As each program generated solutions for company leadership action, assignments were updated to correspond with the latest developments.

In 2005, as directors reporting to the vice presidents enrolled in the program, the HR team developed a team assignment that examined the challenging question of how the company could maintain a talent pipe-line of engineers and scientists as well as retain the knowledge of the retirees.

Ian Ziskin, chief human resources and administrative officer, was passionate about the issue and wanted to use it in the course, but he was concerned that participants would view the topic as an "HR problem" and therefore would not fully engage in the exercise. In the end, he decided to move ahead, knowing that line directors probably knew the problems of recruiting and retention as well as the HR staff and could develop realistic solutions.

"We saw a great opportunity to enlist the help of our leaders in building the best workforce and workplace," says Ziskin. "Using the LEADING program to address the issue got them involved, provided us with a multitude of ideas to help find solutions, and gave us an early start over our competitors in addressing the issue."

Human Capital Management

In November 2005, Northrop Grumman added human capital management to the program to help create a new human capital strategy. Key elements of the approach included:

◆ Sending participants a white paper describing the human capital situation before the class

◆ Incorporating a segment on the company's strategic challenges, including the role that human capital plays in achieving a competitive advantage

◆ Following the strategy presentation with details of Northrop Grumman 's current and projected human capital situation

◆ Facilitating teams to develop ideas rapidly

◆ Reporting recommendations to key executives that resulted in corporation-wide initiatives

◆ Supporting grassroots initiatives inspired by the week's involvement

Rapid Idea Generation

The teams were asked, "What innovative solutions should the company take to minimize the risk of human capital drain and to maintain a competitive advantage?"

The topic is complex and the possibilities for action are numerous, yet the time allotted to work on this issue could be only a few hours out of the entire week. Thus, facilitators worked with each team using a facilitation design that was based on the Creative Problem Solving approach created by Alex Osborn and Sid Pames.

This design allowed course participants to "mess around" with the data before generating solutions. Participants began by privately capturing their thoughts and ideas after the presentation, and then spent time getting to know each other and creating a team charter. During a brainstorming session, the team captured ideas, thoughts, and concerns before choosing a topic or forming the elements of a vision strategy.

During the week, the team developed ideas on how to address the human capital management issue. The company wanted both evolutionary and revolutionary solutions, which forced the facilitators to lead the teams in both directions. A brief description of the work of Michael Kirton, developer of the Kirton Adaption-Innovation Inventory, helped participants use techniques leading to many evolutionary and revolutionary ideas. Participants then discussed and selected the ideas they wished to develop in depth, working up more detail so that corporate teams could consider each recommendation for further work.

The subgroups presented their recommendations to each other for critical comments. Each team selected its top two ideas and coordinated with the other teams to provide an integrated presentation. On the final morning, the teams presented their best ideas to company executives using supportive documentation.

Evolving Assignments

The action learning assignment was enhanced based on the lessons learned from each class and the changes that occurred as the organization acted on recommendations from each team.

In 2006, Northrop Grumman changed the assignment by noting specific areas to explore, such as retaining experienced employees or enlarging and attracting the pool of college graduates. The topics were refined later in the year, after Ziskin chartered HR teams to use the directors' recommendations and data from employee focus groups to identify the top four strategic needs, a vision for each need, and specific implementation initiatives.

Accordingly, the HR executives asked the directors to recommend visions and initiatives for the four strategies. The directors could see how the input of earlier programs had shaped this strategic direction, which in turn helped them create more specific proposals.

These evolving assignments also helped the directors identify contributions they could personally make in bridging the talent gap. In fact, at the end of each program, every director listed specific actions to take back to their jobs. In late 2006, Northrop Grumman surveyed program graduates to find out what they had done to address the human capital challenge.

Substantial Results

An in-house survey of director-level respondents revealed that, beyond the corporate HR initiatives, the ideas from the teams generated action items for corporate leaders. Nearly every survey respondent had some initiative to report. These ideas have empowered the leaders to make changes to the company's culture and vision. For example, one leader committed to having a diverse slate of candidates for every job opening regardless of the pressure to hire quickly. Another leader found resources in another sector—that is, across the One Northrop Grumman initiative—to help her write a new business proposal, thus strengthening the proposal and developing people across the corporation.

"I have been working to ensure that my employees are challenged and satisfied in their current positions," one director wrote. "If they are not, I have actively worked to address their concerns and, in some instances, have assisted them in finding a new position in the company instead of losing them to a competitor."

Thus, the results of this action-learning component of the LEADING program were substantial. The directors increasingly act as "One Northrop Grumman," and as they involve the people who report to them, there are more engaged employees with an understanding of the company's vision as well as the importance of improving company performance. Like Dragojlovic and his team, Northrop Grumman's leaders are bridging the talent gap with their own management action and not waiting for someone else to initiate change.

CASE STUDY 3

The Utility Leaders of the Future

By E. Parson

SOURCE: From "The Utility Leaders of the Future," *Transmission & Distribution World* 58, no. 1 (2006): 56–62. Reprinted with permission.

If you take a close look at the demographic profile of employees at Oklahoma Gas & Electric (OG&E, Oklahoma City), the portrait is not unlike many utilities around the country—plenty of experienced engineers in their 50s and 60s, a small group of 40-somethings, an even smaller band of late 20- and 30-year-olds, and a handful of recent grads, many of whom were not specifically educated as "power" engineers. This reality makes Terry Henry's position as leader of strategy and electric services at OG&E even more challenging. He knows what these numbers will mean for his workforce sooner than later.

That's why he's already formulated a contingency plan to develop replacements for the large group of OG&E employees facing retirement in the next decade or so. "Getting new employees is only one of the challenges," Henry says. "Retaining and planning future work with this mobile generation of young engineers is difficult without really knowing who is going to be here five, ten, or twenty years down the road."

To help deal with these unknowns, OG&E recently changed its recruitment and retention approach by developing a program that changes the dynamic of traditional entry-level engineering positions in order to more effectively attract and retain young talent. "We've taken some of the simplistic work out of the traditional entry-level jobs, such as going out into the field and driving stakes into the ground and doing job sketches and estimates," Henry says. Instead, OG&E has developed a plan whereby engineers come in and spend the first year learning the fundamentals of distribution. Next comes a year working in strategic planning and business development. After a taste of the management track, they rotate into technical design jobs in transmission, control, and system protection.

Similar to OG&E, the average employee is 48 years old at National Grid (Westborough, Massachusetts), one of the world's largest utilities with electricity transmission systems in the northeastern United States that distributes electricity to approximately 3.3 million customers. Characterizing the looming engineering shortage as a "simmering crisis," Chris Root, senior vice president of T&D technical services at National Grid, knows his company must act now to combat the pending employment void that seems to be inevitable.

According to Root, falling employment projections are not the industry's only problem. "Because the nation's transmission systems were mostly built in the 1960s, there's no question that more work is on the way," he says. "At some point, somebody is eventually going to have to do something about that, which will cause a pent-up demand for potential work that will be necessary going forward. So, not only are we going to have to hire people to replace the people that are on the payroll today, but we're going to need more of the existing population."

A Look Inside the Engineering Shortage

According to the most recent data from Engineering Trends, a firm specializing in the study and analysis of engineering education, undergraduate first-year enrollments for engineers has declined 2.5 percent since fall 2002, and total full-time enrollments declined 0.4 percent in the fall of 2004. Since fall 2001, part-time undergraduate enrollments have declined 16.4 percent. Richard Heckel, founder and technical director of Engineering Trends, expects bachelor's degree declines to begin in the next few years.

According to Sakis Melioupoulis, a professor at the School of Electrical & Computer Engineering at Georgia Institute of Technology, not only is the number of students who are going into power decreasing but so is the number of universities with power programs. "There has definitely been a downward trend that hit bottom about three or four years ago," he says. "Since then, we've seen a slight increase but not to previous levels."

What's causing the drop in engineering enrollment? Most industry veterans agree the problem lies within. "I think we have a PR issue, in that people do not think the utility industry has great significant technical challenges," Root says. "College graduates look at us and see poles and wires, and don't realize there are things like automation, computer control, and sophisticated asset management systems out there."

Recruiting Today's Talent

After losing fourteen engineers in a little more than one year in the late 1990s to the telecommunications boom, Root says National Grid got a big wake-up call. "The electrical engineers we lost were younger and more mobile," he says.

In many cases, these companies hire for the short term, so they may pay big money and dangle incentives such as stock options to attract people. "Losing that many engineers in such a short period of time made us really think about how we attract and keep engineers," Root admits. As a result, National Grid beefed up its collegiate recruiting program, visiting eighteen schools per year and targeting the best students, as well as diversity candidates. But the company has not stopped there. It plants the recruitment seed much earlier. "Research has told us that to get people interested in science you really have to start in about third or fourth grade," Root maintains.

National Grid is very active in educating schoolchildren of this age, providing schools with videotapes, materials, and documents for elementary schools. "When you first introduce physical science, you really want to get kids excited because by the time they get into junior high, if they're already turned off by science, there is less of a chance to get them to take advanced science courses such as physics in high school," Root says. "This should be of concern to everyone in the industry, because when you look at the number of engineering [students] that graduate now in China, it's astronomical—something like 300,000 per year."

At OG&E, recruitment efforts were somewhat dormant for a span of almost twenty years. Since it resumed recruiting more aggressively, the company's had great luck attracting topnotch graduates. Not only has the utility doubled the number of campuses it visits from three to six per year but it's also changed the makeup of its recruiting team, now including an HR representative, an experienced engineer, and a younger engineer.

Grooming Generation Y

Zac Hager is one of OG&E's hip new hires that go on recruiting trips with hope of speaking potential college kids' language. As a roving engineer, he's been with the company for three years and has already participated in distribution design, regulatory filings, reliability studies, and most recently asset management.

Hager is what you might call a typical Generation Y'er. He is ambitious, outspoken, and eager to learn. Currently following an engineering management path, similar to an engineering MBA degree, Hager is preparing to take the PE exam in a year while pursuing a master of science in engineering and technology management from Oklahoma State University. Characterizing himself as "having no fear," Hager admits there are some truths to the stereotypes his elder engineers may spread about his generation, but he also feels the group is often incorrectly labeled.

"The vice president of my business unit joked one day that I wasn't old enough to realize that I should have fear," Hager says. "I have also been called ambitious and eager because I take advantage of every challenge that is thrown at me. Everyone still believes that my generation is a transient job-hopping bunch, but I believe that the power industry will continue to have people retiring with thirty and forty years of experience with the same company by the time I retire." Having grown up with computers, electronics, and multimedia galore, Hager maintains that most of the differences between the retiring workforce and the new entrants stem from technology.

Recently working on the capital budget, with direction from his boss, Hager's also a computer whiz. "We're using this optimization technique, and no one knew the ins and outs of the new software," Hager explains. "I get into it, start using it, and see things I don't like about it. So I'm going in and changing things from the back end, such as how you enter information into the program. This seems foreign to everybody else, but this is what we did in school."

Working in the utility business for three decades, OG&E's Henry says the generational differences do exist, but he maintains that the industry must embrace change in order to move forward. This genre's trademark seems to be assertiveness, not arrogance. "Today's graduates are definitely more informed and more savvy, as they have a lot more information at their fingertips," Henry says. "In this environment, it's not uncommon for undergraduate engineers today to have already sampled two or three job assignments before they even get to graduation." Raciel Leiva, one of Melioupoulis's undergraduate students, is a good case in point. As a senior this year, he's already worked in a research capacity on campus, as well as completed a hands-on internship. "The people at [this utility] have an idea of what the power system has been for the last thirty years, but they're not really familiar with the new technology coming out in the market," Leiva says. "So it was a great opportunity for me to interact with these engineers and show them what the new technology is and where we want the power systems to be twenty years from now."

Leiva says the reason he's pursuing a career in electric power is that he wants to own his own company someday. "I wouldn't be afraid to sit down with the supervisor of a substation designer and say, 'this is wrong,'" he says. "Most of my friends would do the same thing. [Experienced engineers] have to accept the fact that this is new technology and listen to us. Understandably, it's really hard for the old engineers to switch to a new type of technology after thirty years of doing things a certain way."

Although everyone wants to make the highest salary possible, most recent grads like Leiva agree that their decision to take a first job is about more than money. It's all about the package—salary, benefits, opportunity, and location. Hager says he's also noticed a growing trend toward family concerns. "I, like others my age, don't want to live in the workaholic America," he says. "I want to go to work and put in a hard, honest eight- to nine-hour day, and then I want to go home and be left alone. Many of us are more than willing to put in longer hours if it is really needed, but it can't be a consistent trend.

"Quality of work diminishes by the time you have worked ten hours, and attitudes and retention worsen with each continuous day of extended work hours," Hager continues. "Don't bother calling me on Sunday morning because I'll be at church. When I'm on vacation, I won't be checking e-mail. Everyone wants to know what happened to values in today's society, but the truth is they start in the home. Utilities should encourage community involvement and allow workers to spend time with their families. I will be there for my kids—when I have them—like my folks were there for me."

Training and Retaining Today's Talent

Given the shortage of technical talent, it seems there is no easy cure for the utility industry to solve the looming engineering crisis. However, many have opted to develop creative, customized solutions.

The United Kingdom has developed one such innovative approach. Andrew Cross, director of development and training at EA Technology, is part of the team behind an initiative called the Power Academy (www .iee.org/poweracademy) to meet engineering staffing needs for the industry's future. Similar to a scholarship in the United States, this program is available through four universities in England, Scotland, and Northern Ireland. Ten utilities and six manufacturers/consultancy firms agree to sponsor one or more students who are studying power engineering by paying for their education and guaranteeing them summer employment as an intern. Last year, forty-five students joined the program, but Cross expects the program to reach more than ninety in 2006. He also commented that the Academy universities have already seen increases in the number and quality of students applying for these electrical engineering courses. EA Technology's sponsored students are expected to come on-board as full-time employees after graduation.

Root follows a similar approach at National Grid. His company's philosophy is: If you can't find 'em, make 'em. "We found that we had a very difficult time attracting anyone higher than a bachelor-level degree, and we had a number of jobs that needed more sophistication," he says. "We couldn't find master's degreed people at all, so we partnered with Worcester Polytechnic Institute and started offering a certificate in power system management." National Grid selects ten qualified candidates from a pool of applicants and sends them back to school for one year to take graduate-level courses to ensure specialized training among its workforce. "It was a difficult year for them because it was a sacrifice," Root says. "The company paid 100 percent of their costs, gave them every third Friday off to go to school, but they had to agree to give up every third Saturday to attend classes as well. We felt that if we gave up Friday, they could give up Saturday."

So far, the utility has put fifty-three people through the program. "By doing this, we created a tremendous increase in the number of technical people in the company than we previously had," Root notes. "Our retention rate of those people has also been extremely good. We've lost only two of them. Although it cost about $10,000 per employee, it's been extremely successful."

Now considering ideas outside of the traditional hiring paradigm, such as signing bonuses and hiring people for contract terms rather than as full-time employees, OG&E's Henry realized that the current employment crisis is mostly self-imposed. Despite the fact that utilities are competing with so many other industries, including communications, computers, manufacturing, and the military, Henry remains optimistic about the future leadership of the industry. "In my mind, the utility industry is invisible to the public, but it's changing—with a lot of new ideas, new technology, and specialization," Henry says. "We just need to tell our story."

Appendix II

An Instrument for Measuring the Strategic Framework for a Technical and Professional Talent Management Program

Directions: Use this instrument to measure the perceptions of people in your organization about how well the organization is meeting, at the strategic level, the unique needs of technical and professional workers through its TTM program. Distribute this survey to decision makers in the organization and have them rate each item in the left-hand column, using the following scale: *0 = Not applicable to the needs of this organization; 1 = the organization does not do this effectively at all; (2) the organization effectively does this on occasion; (3) the organization does this adequately and regularly; and (4) the organization always does this effectively.* There are no right or wrong answers; the goal is to measure perceptions. Compile the results and total the score, and then rate the results using the scale at the end.

		How Often Does the Organization Adhere to this Characteristic?					
	Strategic Characteristics of Effective TTM Programs	Not applicable	Never does this	Sometimes does this	Regularly does this	Always does this	*Notes or Comments*
		0	1	2	3	4	
1	Established measurable goals to be achieved by a TTM program	0	1	2	3	4	
2	Clarified the roles to be played by each group	0	1	2	3	4	
3	Established how stakeholders will be accountable for achieving the program goals	0	1	2	3	4	
4	Identified the work processes critical to the organization's success	0	1	2	3	4	
5	Defined the present work duties of important technical and professional workers	0	1	2	3	4	
6	Recognized the technical competencies of important technical and professional workers	0	1	2	3	4	
7	Determined a way to pinpoint the workers who possess the most valuable knowledge	0	1	2	3	4	
8	Estimated the risk of loss of workers who possess the most valuable knowledge	0	1	2	3	4	
9	Aligned strategic plans with future talent needs	0	1	2	3	4	
10	Implemented the program by recruiting, developing, and retaining people with special knowledge	0	1	2	3	4	

		How Often Does the Organization Adhere to this Characteristic?					
Strategic Characteristics of Effective TTM Programs		Not applicable	Never does this	Sometimes does this	Regularly does this	Always does this	*Notes or Comments*
		0	1	2	3	4	
11	Has practical ways to transfer knowledge to less experienced people	0	1	2	3	4	
12	Has practical ways to evaluate the continuing results of the TTM program	0	1	2	3	4	

Total _____

Scoring

11 to 12   Your organization appears to have an effective strategic framework to support a technical talent management program.

7 to 10   Your organization has many elements of an effective strategic framework to support a technical talent management program. Direct attention to the missing elements.

4 to 6   Your organization is not focusing attention on the potential, and perhaps disastrous, loss of technical and professional workers. Take action!

0 to 3   Your organization is failing in its efforts to attract, develop, and retain HiPros, as well as to transfer their knowledge to less experienced workers.

Appendix III

An Instrument for Measuring Technical and Professional Talent Management as Enacted on a Daily (Tactical) Basis

Directions: Use this instrument to measure the perceptions of people in your organization about how well managers, in general, successfully manage, on a daily basis (that is, the tactical level), the unique needs of technical and professional workers through a TTM program. Distribute this survey to the appropriate people and ask them to rate each item listed in the left-hand column as follows: *0 = Not applicable to the needs of this organization; 1 = the managers in this organization do not do this effectively at all; 2 = the managers in this organization effectively do this on occasion; 3 = the managers in this organization do this adequately and* *regularly;* and *4 = the managers in this organization always do this effectively.* There are no right or wrong answers in any absolute sense; the purpose here is to measure perceptions. Compile the results, total the scores, and compare to the rating scale at the end.

Tactical Characteristics of Effective TTM Programs	How Often Do Managers in the Organization Adhere to this Characteristic?					*Notes or Comments*
	Not applicable	Never does this	Sometimes does this	Regularly does this	Always does this	
	0	1	2	3	4	
1 Know their daily role in the organization's TTM program	0	1	2	3	4	
2 Work on a daily basis within established accountabilities for each attracting, developing, and retaining technical and professional talent	0	1	2	3	4	
3 Work on a daily basis within established accountabilities to facilitate transfer of valuable knowledge	0	1	2	3	4	
4 Individually measured for how well they carry out their roles on a daily basis	0	1	2	3	4	
5 Participate in improving ways managers can contribute to the success of the TTM program on a daily basis	0	1	2	3	4	
6 Use systematic approaches to encourage knowledge transfer	0	1	2	3	4	
7 Are evaluated on their contributions to the success of the program	0	1	2	3	4	

Total _____

New Employees Up to Speed in Half the Time (New York: John Wiley, 2009).

Chapter 4

1. C. Gonzalez, "The Role of Blended Learning in the World of Technology." See www.unt.edu/benchmarks/archives/2004/september04.

2. William Rothwell, *The Workplace Learner: How to Align Training Initiatives with Individual Learning Competencies* (New York: AMACOM, 2002).

3. See William J. Rothwell, M. Butler, C. Maldonado, D. Hunt, K. Peters, J. Li., and J. Stern, *Handbook of Training Technology: An Introductory Guide to Facilitating Learning with Technology—from Planning Through Evaluation* (San Francisco: Pfeiffer & Co., 2006).

4. Ruth Colvin Clark, *Developing Technical Training: A Structured Approach for Developing Classroom and Computer-Based Instructional Materials*, 3rd ed. (San Francisco: Pfeiffer, 2007); William J. Rothwell and Joseph Benkowski, *Building Effective Technical Training: How to Develop Hard Skills in Organizations* (San Francisco: Jossey-Bass/Pfeiffer, 2002).

5. David D. Dubois and William J. Rothwell, *The Competency Toolkit.* 2 vols. (Amherst, Mass.: HRD Press, 2000).

6. William J. Rothwell and Jim Graber, *Competency-Based Training Basics* (Alexandria, Va.: ASTD Press, 2010).

7. Ibid.

8. William J. Rothwell and H. C. Kanzanas, *Improving On-the-Job Training: How to Establish and Operate a Comprehensive OJT Program*, 2nd ed. (San Francisco: Pfeiffer and Company, 2004).

9. Joseph A. Raelin, *Work-Based Learning: Bridging Knowledge and Action in the Workplace* (San Francisco: Jossey-Bass, 2008).

10. William J. Rothwell, *The Action Learning Guidebook: A Real-Time Strategy for Problem-Solving, Training Design, and Employee Development* (San Francisco: Jossey-Bass/Pfeiffer, 1999).

11. Stanley Poduch, *Exploring the Experiences of Technical Coaches Using Rules-of-Thumb.* Unpublished Ph.D. dissertation, Pennsylvania State University, 2010.

12. William J. Rothwell, *The Self-Directed On-the-Job Learning Workshop* (Amherst, Mass.: Human Resource Development Press, 1996).

Chapter 5

1. Joan Fitzgerald, *Moving Up in the New Economy: Career Ladders for U.S. Workers* (Ithaca, N.Y.: ILR Press, 2006).

2. The most detailed treatment is found in Gary W. Carter, Kevin W. Cook, and David W. Dorsey, *Career Paths: Charting Courses to Success for Organizations and Their Employees* (New York: Wiley-Blackwell, 2009).

3. Ted Leung and Jim Robertson, "Dual Career Ladders." Accessed April 16, 2010; http://www.cincomsmalltalk.com/userblogs/rad emers/blogView?showComments = true&entry = 3253517059.

Chapter 6

1. Bernard L., Rosenbaum, "Leading Today's Professional," *Research Technology Management* 34, no. 2 (1991): 30–35.

2. See William J. Rothwell, *Effective Succession Planning: Ensuring Leadership Continuity and Building Talent from Within*, 4th ed. (New York: AMACOM, 2010).

3. Laurence J. Peter and Raymond Hull, *The Peter Principle: Why Things Always Go Wrong*, reprint (New York: HarperBusiness, 2009).

4. Monica Favia, *An Initial Competency Model for Sales Managers at Fifteen B2B Organizations.* Unpublished doctoral dissertation, Pennsylvania State University, 2010.

5. J. Daniel Sherman, "Technical Supervision and Turnover Among Engineers and Technicians: Influencing Factors in the Work Environment," *Group and Organization Management* 14, no. 4 (1989): 411–21.

6. Gene Dixon, "Can We Lead and Follow?" *Engineering Management Journal* 21, no. 1 (2009): 34–41; Jerry C. Meyer and Gregg F. Martin, "Join the Campaign: Engineer Leader Technical Competency," *Engineer* 38, no. 1 (2008): 4–7; Anne Milkovich, *Management Bytes: Ten Essential Skills for Technical Managers* (Roseville, Calif.: Penmarin Books, 2005).

7. See William J. Rothwell, "Organization Retention Assessment," in *The 2007 Pfeiffer Annual: Consulting*, ed. E. Beich (San Francisco: Pfeiffer, 2007), pp. 177–88.

8. Julie Zinn and Raed Haddad, "The New Essential Skills," *Industrial Engineer* 39, no. 5 (2007): 35–39.

9. E. Casey Wardynski, David S. Lyle, and William E. Mohr, "Developing an Engineer Leader Technical Competency Strategy: Accessing, Developing, Employing, and Retaining Talent," *Engineer* 38, no. 2 (2008): 20.

10. S. Crabtree, "Getting Personal in the Workplace: Are Negative Relationships Squelching Productivity in Your Company?" *Gallup Management Journal*, 2007; http://www.govleaders.org/gallup_article _getting_personal.htm.

11. Henry Sauermann and Wesley M. Cohen, "Motivated to Innovate," *MIT Sloan Management Review* 50, no. 3 (2009): 24ff.

12. Ibid., p. 24.

13. William J. Rothwell, J. Stavros, R. Sullivan, and A. Sullivan, Eds.,

Practicing Organization Development: A Guide for Leading Change, 3rd ed. (San Francisco: Pfeiffer, 2010).

14. See Gallup Study, "Engaged Employees Inspire Company Innovation," October 2006; http://gmj.gallup.com/content/24880/gallup-study-engaged-employees-inspire-company.aspx.

15. David Gliddon, *Forecasting a Behavioral Competency Model for Innovation Leaders Using a Modified Delphi Technique.* Unpublished Ph.D. dissertation, Pennsylvania State University, 2006.

16. See Cynthia A. Lengnick-Hall, "Innovation and Competitive Advantage: What We Know and What We Need to Learn," *Journal of Management*, June 1992; accessed April 18, 2010; http://findarticles.com/p/articles/mi_m4256/is_n2_v18/ai_12720969/

17. Gliddon, *Forecasting*, p. 85.

18. The worksheet is based on the approach suggested by goal analysis, made famous by Robert F. Mager in his classic *Goal Analysis: How to Clarify Your Goals So You Can Actually Achieve Them*, 3rd ed. (Atlanta: CEP Press, 1997).

19. William J. Rothwell, *The Manager's Guide to Maximizing Employee Potential* (New York: AMACOM, 2010).

Chapter 7

1. The classic is, of course, Ikujiro Nonaka, *The Knowledge-Creating Company*, Harvard Business Review Classics (Cambridge, Mass.: Harvard Business School Press, 2008).

2. Wlliam J. Rothwell and Stanley Poduch, "Introducing Technical (Not Managerial) Succession Planning," *Public Personnel Management 33*, no. 4 (2004): 405–20.

Chapter 8

1. See http://www.supershareware.com/knowledge-management -group-free/.

2. The list that follows is based in part on William J. Rothwell, "Knowledge Transfer: 12 Strategies for Succession Management," *IPMA-HR News*, February 2004, pp. 10–12.

3. See http://www.att.com/gen/corporate-citizenship?pid = 11547.

4. The program is described at http://www.performancesolutions.nc .gov/developmentInitiatives/KnowledgeTransfer/index.aspx, accessed April 12, 2010.

5. Ettienne Wenger, Richard McDermott, William M. Snyder, *Cultivating Communities of Practice* (Cambridge, Mass.: Harvard Business School Press, 2002).

6. See, for instance, Synthis at http://www.facebook.com/pages/Synthis -Awesome-Process-Documentation-Software/ 328261730907?_fb_noscript = 1.

7. See, for instance, Charlotte Long, *Job Aids for Everyone* (Amherst, Mass.: HRD Press, 2005); Allison Rossett and Lisa Schafer, *Job Aids and Performance Support: Moving From Knowledge in the Classroom to Knowledge Everywhere* (San Francisco: Pfeiffer, 2006); Joe Willmore, *Job Aids Basics* (Alexandria, Va.: ASTD Press, 2006).

8. See Marcie Begleiter, *From Word to Image: Storyboarding and the Filmmaking Process*, 2nd ed. (Studio City, Calif.: Michael Wiese Productions, 2010); Giuseppe Cristiano, *Storyboard Design Course: Principles, Practice, and Techniques* (Hauppauge, N.Y.: Barron's Educational Series, 2007).

9. See, for instance, Tammy D. Allen, Lisa M. Finkelstein, and Mark L. Poteet, *Designing Workplace Mentoring Programs: An Evidence-Based Approach* (New York: Wiley-Blackwell, 2009); Norman Cohen, *A*

Step-by-Step Guide to Starting an Effective Mentoring Program (Amherst, Mass.: HRD Press, 2000); Lois J. Zachary, *The Mentor's Guide: Facilitating Effective Learning Relationships* (San Francisco: Jossey-Bass, 2000).

10. See, for instance, Evelyn Clark, "Around the Corporate Campfire: How Great Leaders Use Stories to Inspire Success" (Chester, England: C&C Publishing, 2004); Stephen Denning, *The Leader's Guide to Storytelling: Mastering the Art and Discipline of Business Narrative* (San Francisco: Jossey-Bass, 2005); Annette Simmons, *The Story Factor*, 2nd rev. ed. (New York: Basic Books, 2006).

11. See Robert C. Camp, *Benchmarking: The Search for Industry Best Practices That Lead to Superior Performance* (New York: Productivity Press, 2006); Tim Stapenhurst, *The Benchmarking Book: A How-To Guide to Best Practice for Managers and Practitioners* (Burlington, Mass.: Butterworth-Heinemann, 2009); accessed April 12, 2010; http://en.wikipedia.org/wiki/Help.

12. Daniel Barrett, *Mediawiki (Wikipedia and Beyond)* (Santa Rosa, Calif.: O'Reilly Media, 2008); Andrew Dalby, *The World and Wikipedia: How We Are Editing Reality* (Somerset, England: Siduri Books, 2009); Dan Woods and Peter Theony, *Wikis for Dummies* (New York: For Dummies, 2007).

13. See http://www.mindtools.com/pages/article/newISS_01.htm.

14. Juanita Brown, David Isaacs, and the World Cafe Community, *The World Cafe: Shaping Our Futures Through Conversations That Matter* (San Francisco: Berrett-Koehler Publishers, 2005).

15. For more on GDSS technology, see Frada Burstein and Clyde W. Holsapple, *Handbook on Decision Support Systems 1: Basic Themes* (New York: Springer, 2008); ICON Group International, *Decision Support Systems: Webster's Timeline History, 1966–2007* (San Diego: ICON Group International, 2009); Frederic P. Miller, Agnes F. Vandome, and John McBrewster, *Group Decision Support Systems* (Mauritius: Alphascript, 2009).

16. See A. R. Tyler, *Expert Systems Research Trends* (Hauppauge, N.Y.: Nova Science Publishers, 2007) and also the Wikipedia page on expert systems at http://en.wikipedia.org/wiki/Expert_system.

17. See David E. Stone and Jan C. Potter, *Developing Electronic Performance Support Systems* (Boca Raton, Fla.: CRC Press, 2010).

18. William J. Rothwell, Harvey Sterns, Diane Spokus, and Joel Reaser, *Working Longer: New Strategies for Managing, Training, and Retaining Older Employees* (New York: AMACOM, 2008).

Chapter 9

1. Tom Bately, "Management of Professional Engineers in New Zealand," *Journal of European Industrial Training* 22, no.7 (1998): 309–12.

2. Ming-Tien Tsai, Chen-Chung Chen, and Chao-Wei Chin, "Knowledge Workers' Interpersonal Skills and Innovation Performance: An Empirical Study of Taiwanese High-Tech Industrial Workers," *Social Behavior and Personality: An International Journal* 3, no. 1 (2010): 115–26.

3. Elliott Jacques, *Time-Span Handbook: The Use of Time-Span of Discretion to Measure the Level of Work in Employment Roles and to Arrange an Equitable Payment Structure* (London: Heinemann, 1964).

4. See http://www.ask.com/bar?q = How + long + is + the + time + between + researching + a + new + drug + and + bringing + it + to + market%3F&page = 1&qsrc = 2106&dm = all&ab = 2&u = http %3A%2F%2Fwww.time.com%2Ftime%2Fmagazine%2Farticle%2F0 %2C9171%2C404241%2C00.html&sg = M201%2FOLotRP4Tp8P 8Ef%2BxWzz%2BEFTnVq0rmI9cpnXB8s%3D&tsp = 1270928 761532; accessed April 13, 2010.

5. William J. Rothwell, "Ethics and the Role of HR," *People Manager,* March 2010, pp. 6–8.

6. C. K. Prahalad and G. Hamel, G., "The Core Competence of the Corporation," *Harvard Business Review* 68, no. 3 (1990): 79–91.

7. M. Buckingham and D. Clifton, *Now, Discover Your Strengths* (New York: Free Press, 2001.)

8. Tom Rath, *StrengthsFinder 2.0: A New and Upgraded Edition of the Online Test from Gallup's Now, Discover Your Strengths* (Washington, D.C.: Gallup Press, 2007).

Index

About the Author

William J. Rothwell, Ph.D., SPHR, is Professor of Learning and Performance in the Workforce Education and Development Program, Department of Learning and Performance Systems, at The Pennsylvania State University, University Park campus. In that capacity, he heads a graduate program in learning and performance. He has authored, co-authored, edited, or co-edited 300 books, book chapters, and articles—including 68 books. Before arriving at Penn State in 1993, he had 20 years' work experience as a training director in government and in business. He has also worked as a consultant for more than 40 multinational corporations, including Motorola, General Motors, and Ford. In 2004, he earned the Graduate Faculty Teaching Award at Pennsylvania State University, given to the best graduate faculty member on the 23 campuses of the

Penn State system. His train-the-trainer programs have won global awards for excellence from Motorola University and from Linkage, Inc. His recent books include *Competency-Based Training Basics* (ASTD, 2010), *Manager's Handbook for Maximizing Employee Potential: Quick and Easy Strategies to Develop Talent Every Day* (AMACOM, 2010), *Effective Succession Planning: Ensuring Leadership Continuity and Building Talent from Within*, 4th ed. (AMACOM, 2010), *Practicing Organization Development*, 3rd ed. (Pfeiffer, 2010), *Basics of Adult Learning* (ASTD, 2009), *HR Transformation* (Davies-Black, 2008), and *Working Longer: New Strategies for Managing, Training, and Retaining Older Employees* (AMACOM, 2008). Many of his books have been translated into other languages, including Chinese, Russian, Vietnamese, and Korean. A frequent conference keynoter and seminar presenter in the United States and many other countries, he can be reached by e-mail at wjr9@psu.edu.